LOUISIANA'S
NO MAN'S LAND

LOUISIANA'S
NO MAN'S LAND

A HISTORY OF
OUTLAWS & OPPORTUNITY

SCOTT DeBOSE

THE
History
PRESS

Published by The History Press
Charleston, SC
www.historypress.com

First published 2024

Manufactured in the United States

ISBN 9781467155366

Library of Congress Control Number: 2023940770

Notice: The information in this book is true and complete to the best of our knowledge. It is offered without guarantee on the part of the author or The History Press. The author and The History Press disclaim all liability in connection with the use of this book.

CONTENTS

I would like to dedicate this work to the descendants of the settlers of No Man's Land who continue to tell the stories of the past and help keep the memories alive. Without their dedication to the past, we would not know the rich history and culture of this region.

As always, I want to thank my family for their help and support, especially my wife, Courtney, for reading and rereading drafts of this work and her encouragement.

INTRODUCTION

Most people think that the Louisiana Purchase was a smooth transaction in which France handed over a massive territory to the United States and everything went peacefully. Few people realize that the Louisiana Purchase almost started a war between the United States and Spain; that a former vice president and the commander of the United States Army hatched a plot to create their own empire west of the Mississippi River; or that in all the wheeling and dealing over the boundary, a forty-mile-wide strip of land got left out of the Louisiana Purchase, and for almost twenty years, the people living there had no country to call home. This so-called No Man's Land was not just a place for outlaws, but it also attracted many settlers who wanted to start a new life and cultural groups looking to maintain their identities.

What is No Man's Land? This is a question that professional historians, anthropologists, folklorists and residents still debate. If you are not from western Louisiana, your first thought may be that "No Man's Land" refers to the space of ground between the two opposing trench lines in World War I. But for those from western Louisiana or who are studying Louisiana history, it is the strip of land between the Sabine River and Arroyo Hondo/Calcasieu River left out of the Louisiana Purchase. The area went by many names: the Neutral Ground, the Neutral Strip, No Man's Land, the Sabine Strip, the Free State of Sabine and the Devil's Playground. Most of the stories, legends and family histories about the area have more of a connection to the geography and location of the region than to a historical era. An outlaw story from the 1880s or a settler story from 1840 are both equally connected to No Man's Land, even though neither took place during the historical Neutral Ground Era. In a historical sense, it is the western part of Louisiana that was left out of the Louisiana Purchase and, from 1806 to 1821, was not part of any country, since neither Spain nor the United States could settle or station troops in the region. From a cultural standpoint, the region's time as a neutral ground has had a lasting effect on the development of the culture of the area—one that is very different from the rest of Louisiana. This book will cover periods both before and after 1806–21, looking at the time spent from about 1700 to the 1940s to better understand both the origins of No Man's Land and the lasting effect it had on cultural development in the region. No Man's Land is a place where cultures met and mixed over time. Several Native American groups called the region home before the arrival of the first Europeans, and more Native American groups arrived over time, mixing with the French and Spanish. Later came Americans from several different states, and all these groups mixed together to create a culture different from anywhere else in the state.

This work looks at the origin of the Neutral Ground, the historical Neutral Ground Era, the settlement of the region after it became part of the United States and the efforts to bring law and order to No Man's Land. Much of the history of the region is recorded in oral histories and legends, which makes confirming details of events difficult. Many of these oral histories do not specify dates, making placing them in chronological order challenging. This work attempts to group events into a rough timeline based on the details of the stories and place them as either happening before the historical Neutral Ground Era or during the period before or after the region officially became part of the United States. It is not the purpose of this work to prove or disprove the legends of No Man's Land, as some of the legends are as important to the cultural development of the region as the historical facts, although details that are less likely to be historically accurate or stories of which multiple versions exist are labeled as such, when possible. The term *No Man's Land* is used throughout the work more to define the geographical region than to identify a specific period. The names of many settlers are listed in this work; however, this is not intended as an exhaustive list, and more focus is placed on the names of pre–Civil War settlers, as lists of settlers in the post–Civil War era are easier to access. Lastly, this work is designed as an overview, and many great stories, historical events, town histories and family stories had to be left out due to space limitations.

CHAPTER 1

SETTING THE STAGE FOR THE NEUTRAL STRIP

THE LOUISIANA PURCHASE

With the stroke of a pen, the size of the United States doubled. However, neither the seller nor the buyer really knew what was in the territory. It would take decades to work out all the details left out of the Louisiana Purchase, and for a time, hundreds of people would be left with no country to call home. Over one hundred years after the purchase, many in Louisiana were still struggling to find a cultural identity. Not quite French like the rest of Louisiana, not quite Spanish, not fully Americanized and with a mixture of Native American and other cultures thrown in, No Man's Land was a place unlike anywhere else in Louisiana or the United States—made up of a people who had to be completely self-reliant and in constant danger from both strangers and nature who developed a culture all their own and passed it down from generation to generation. This is their story. It is the story of how groups of people survived and thrived in a land with no law or government, one that has always been a borderland between empires and separated from the rest of "civilization" by lack of transportation and communication. Their story, more than just a history of the official Neutral Strip (1806–21), starts hundreds of years before the Louisiana Purchase and continues today.

The year was 1803, and there was panic in the national capital. Word had just reached President Thomas Jefferson that Spain had returned Louisiana to France. Now Napoleon Bonaparte had control of the Mississippi Valley and the Port of New Orleans, which would lead to economic ruin for farmers and merchants in western parts of the United States if Napoleon decided to close the port to American trade. Since 1795, Spain had allowed the United States the "right of deposit," which permitted American farmers and merchants to move goods down the Mississippi River and store them in New Orleans until they could be placed on oceangoing vessels. Jefferson quickly wrote a letter to Robert Livingston, United States minister to France, to find out the details of the agreement. He wrote, "There is on the globe one single spot, the possessor of which is our natural and habitual enemy…it is New Orleans, through which the produce of three-eighths of our territory must pass to market."[1]

Livingston was instructed to try and buy New Orleans; however, for more than a year, the talks went nowhere. Even as the Americans were trying to open negotiations, Napoleon was preparing to send troops to occupy Louisiana. France prepared a large fleet to carry soldiers, settlers and government officials, and Pierre-Clément de Laussat was named colonial prefect and sent ahead of the fleet to New Orleans to prepare for the arrival of French troops.[2]

While the sheer size of the Louisiana territory and the fact that the land had once been French appealed to Napoleon, the most important reason he needed Louisiana was to grow food and timber to supply the island of Santo Domingo and the other "sugar islands" of the Caribbean. These islands provided France an annual income of 150 to 170 million *livres* (or the value of 150 to 170 million pounds of silver) and were considered the wealthiest colony in the world. Every inch of useable ground was needed to grow cash crops such as sugar, and the more food that could be grown off the island meant more land to grow sugarcane and higher profits.[3]

However, before France could physically take possession of Louisiana, events in Europe and the Caribbean would force Napoleon to reconsider the value of Louisiana. Since 1791, Santo Domingo had been in a state of revolt as the enslaved population fought for their freedom from France. After years of hit-and-run guerrilla warfare, during which the rebels' favorite tactic was to sneak into the soldiers' tents and hack them to death with machetes, Napoleon sent an army of about twenty-five thousand soldiers to put down the revolt. While this French army was able to defeat the rebels after a long campaign, the island would have its revenge. Yellow fever broke out among the French, and soon, the twenty-five thousand was reduced to roughly eight thousand, who were weakened by the disease and soon became easy prey for the rebel army. Not even the commander of the expedition was safe: General Leclerc contracted yellow fever and soon died. Napoleon was also aware that England was growing more hostile to his regime and, at any time, might declare war on France to restore the monarchy. In the event of war, Napoleon would not have enough troops to fight in Europe, reconquer Santo Domingo and garrison Louisiana. The vast territory of Louisiana was vulnerable to invasion from the north by British troops in Canada and from the south by land and naval forces from British bases in the Caribbean. While Napoleon probably did not want to sell Louisiana, his inability to protect it and the need for ready cash to finance his armies outweighed any desire for the territory. On April 13, 1803, Livingston was informed that Napoleon wanted to sell not just New Orleans but all the Louisiana territory. While the purchase of that much territory exceeded their authority, both Livingston and the recently arrived James Monroe felt that it was worth the risk to agree to the purchase rather than taking a chance on Napoleon selling New Orleans to someone else— or not selling it at all. They worked out the details for a few days; on May 2, the treaty was agreed to, and by May 8, it had been signed by all parties, being backdated to April 30. However, the boundaries were left very vague: "Louisiana with the same extent it now has in the hands of Spain and that it had when France possessed it." The American ministers pushed for a more detailed boundary line, but when their complaint was brought to Napoleon's attention, he reportedly replied, "If an obscurity did not already exist, it would perhaps be good policy to put one there."[4]

Map of the Louisiana Purchase. *National Archives and Records Administration.*

Left: William C.C. Claiborne. *Right*: James Wilkinson. *Library of Congress.*

The purchase was hotly debated in Congress as being outside of the president's authority, but when the final vote was taken, it passed the Senate twenty-four to seven. To oversee the transfer, William C.C. Claiborne (governor of the Mississippi Territory) and General James Wilkinson (commander of the United States Army) were named commissioners. However, before France could turn Louisiana over to the United States, it first had to take possession of the territory. Even though French colonial prefect Pierre-Clément de Laussat had been in New Orleans since March 26, he was awaiting the arrival of French troops and the rest of the colonial government's officials before he took possession of Louisiana from Spain. When word first reached him about the purchase, Laussat thought it was a trick the Americans were playing and called it an "incredible and impudent falsehood." Laussat was soon informed that the news was true. Instead of preparing to receive Louisiana for the glory of France (and his own personal wealth and influence), Laussat was now forced to make preparations to receive Louisiana only to turn it over to the Americans. In a ceremony held in New Orleans in the Plaza de Armes—Place d'Armes (French) or Plaza de Armas (Spanish)—on November 30, 1803, the Spanish flag was lowered and the French tricolor was raised. The French flag flew over the city for twenty days, after which it was lowered and replaced by the Stars and Stripes when the Americans officially took possession of the territory on December 20, 1803. The Louisiana Purchase was called the largest land deal in history and fifteen future states would be created out of the territory, but there was still no western boundary—and no one in France or the United States seemed to care. However, in Spain, there was great concern.[5]

The Spanish had hoped that French Louisiana would act as a buffer, preventing the western movement of Americans into Spanish-controlled Mexico, whose rich silver mines were a major source of income for the Spanish. The loss of the silver mines would have been a major blow to the

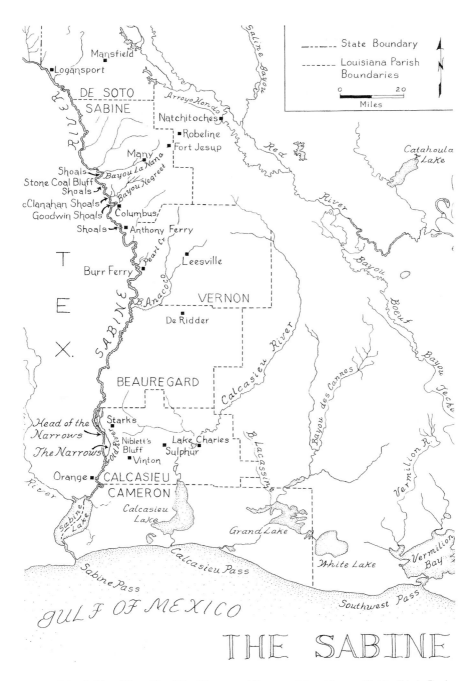

Map of the Sabine River. *From* The Rivers and Bayous of Louisiana, *edited by Edwin Davis (Baton Rouge: Louisiana Education Research Association, 1968).*

Map of the Calcasieu River. *From* The Rivers and Bayous of Louisiana, *edited by Edwin Davis (Baton Rouge: Louisiana Education Research Association, 1968).*

already financially struggling Spanish monarchy. Spain's first action was to try and stop the transfer on the legal grounds that the treaty that transferred the territory from Spain back to France prevented France from selling the territory without Spain's permission. U.S. secretary of state James Madison replied that the United States "can address themselves to the French government to negotiate the acquisition of territories which may suit their interests." The Spanish soon dropped the legal challenge for fear that if they did not turn over Louisiana, the Americans might invade Spanish Florida. Spain now changed strategies and, for the next several years, would do everything possible to limit the size of the Louisiana territory.[6]

Although the official transfer of Louisiana took place in 1803, there were still Spanish garrisons throughout the territory, and General Wilkinson wanted to move quickly to take physical possession of the forts and settlements. However, the departure of U.S. troops was delayed because the Spanish commissioner at New Orleans refused to issue orders to the post commanders to transfer their forts to the Americans until after January 9, 1804. Both Claiborne and Wilkinson were hesitant to transfer troops from New Orleans until the Spanish garrison left the city, which they did not do until after February 20. In January, Wilkinson received reports that the Spanish planned to occupy lands within the territory claimed by the United States, in some places as far as four hundred miles into the territory, and he wanted to occupy the territory as soon as possible. Although Claiborne still opposed the move, Captain Edward D. Turner of the Second United States Infantry Regiment was sent to Natchitoches to take physical possession of the region after additional reinforcements arrived in New Orleans. After a journey of almost three months, U.S. troops arrived in Natchitoches in April 1804. Turner's command consisted of an interpreter, forty-four infantrymen, ten artillerymen, laundresses and Turner's wife and children. His first official duty on arriving was to receive Natchitoches as an American settlement, as well as the rest of North Louisiana, in a ceremony held at Natchitoches on April 26, 1804. The Spanish and French flags were raised and lowered in turn, then the American flag was raised for the first time over Northwest Louisiana.[7]

After the ceremony, the Spanish garrison marched to Nacogdoches, and Turner's troops settled down to the job of garrisoning Natchitoches and choosing a site for a new fort. Turner first looked at the bluffs of Grand Encore, but that site was rejected for two reasons: the site was too far from the town, and the location of the Great Red River Raft (a giant logjam in the river) made a water invasion unlikely. He then selected a site "about

300 yards from the river upon a small knoll in the center of the rear of the village and immediately at the entrance of the Nacogdoches Road from the woods, which it of course guards. The spot is as military a spot as could be found in the vicinity."[8] The site had two small hills, which gave the artillery a line of fire over the river. The Bayou Jacho ran through the back of the site, providing a water source for the post's livestock. Dr. John Sibley, in April 1805, described the fort as being "on a small hill one street from the river and about thirty-three feet higher than the river."[9] The fort and barracks covered about two acres.

Another important point was that the village of Natchitoches was just a few hundred yards from the site, and given that Captain Turner had to serve as the civil magistrate, this was an important consideration. Turner named the post Fort Claiborne in honor of Governor Claiborne. The troops first dug a star-shaped redoubt on the highest ground for their ten to twelve artillery pieces, then they divided into work parties. For the next several months, the men cut timber for the palisades and barracks. Secretary of War Dearborn recommended that the fortifications be built of timber, slightly hewed. Each of the blockhouses was to be two stories and situated to give a good arc of fire, and in the back of the barracks were to be placed portholes, which could be opened and used to fire muskets.

The fort's walls had two bastions on the front (south side of the fort) and two on the rear (north side of the fort). The fort had two gates, the main entrance on the south side and another on the west. However, by 1814, the western gate had been closed by the construction of additional barracks. Both the officers and enlisted soldiers had separate housing, with the officers' quarters facing the front gate and measuring 36 by 116 feet. The officers' quarters had a front and back gallery and included three rooms on each side of the hall. The two enlisted men's barracks each measured 18 by 92 feet and contained five rooms; each was built parallel to each other and to the east and west walls of the fort. Also, inside the stockade was a guardhouse to the left of the gate (when looking from the officers' quarters), which measured 14 by 20 feet, and a magazine on the right side of the gate, which was 14 by 14 feet. Each bastion contained a latrine, which drained outside the fort walls.

Outside the stockade were constructed the support buildings for the fort: the carpenter's shop measured 15 by 22 feet, and the harness and blacksmith shops were contained within a two-room building, 21 by 36 feet. There were, at various times, two kitchens, a temporary hospital and dispensary, a stable, a blockhouse and various other workshops. There was also a garden and a cemetery, which by 1818 contained about two hundred graves. Minor

An 1814 map of Louisiana with the approximate location of No Man's Land highlighted. *Courtesy of the Louisiana State Museum.*

additions were made to the fort from time to time, such as arbors to protect the sentinels from the sun.[10] With most of the construction done, Fort Claiborne's garrison settled into the routines of frontier life; however, the frontier would not stay quiet for long.

The Spanish may have left Louisiana, but that did not mean they had given up on regaining at least some of the territory; in fact, Spain still held territory to both the east and west of Louisiana, with large army and naval forces in both Mexico and Florida. During 1804, a royal committee met in Madrid to discuss the boundary question. The committee agreed that the best option was to limit the Americans to the smallest area of the Louisiana Purchase as possible. The Spanish plan would be to limit the Americans to the east of the Red River and to only the southernmost part of the Mississippi Valley. Spanish officials began preparing for a possible war with the United States, ordering the Spanish fleet in Havana to be ready to blockade Washington, the mouth of the Mississippi and other key ports and rivers. Additional troops were sent to North America, fortifications were strengthened and new forts were built in Texas and Florida. At the same time that Spanish officials were debating how to limit the size of the Louisiana Purchase, officials in the Jefferson administration were coming to the conclusion that the purchase included not only Louisiana and the Midwest but Spanish Texas as well.[11]

Spain soon began sending patrols across the Sabine River and establishing outposts. Late in 1805, Spanish troops set up outposts at Bayou Pierre, at Nana and near the site of Los Adaes, which had been the colonial capital of Spanish Texas in the 1700s. The American response in January 1806 was to order Major Moses Porter, who had assumed command of Fort Claiborne on his arrival in Natchitoches, to open communications with his Spanish counterpart, Rodriguez, at Nacogdoches to get assurance that no acts of violence would be committed. Porter was also instructed to patrol the Sabine River and repel any invasion but to avoid bloodshed, if possible. Rodriguez replied that his troops were only there to stop illegal trade in contraband and horses but that it was his duty to patrol to the Arroyo Hondo. Porter ordered Captain Turner with a force of 60 men to expel the Spanish at Adaes, which was easily done, since the Spanish only had 51 soldiers stationed there. However, Spain was gathering over 1,600 troops in Texas, with 700 en route to the Sabine River. It was at this critical juncture that America would face not only the possibility of a war with an international superpower but also a conspiracy led by a former vice president that threatened to tear the young republic apart.

CHAPTER 2

CONSPIRACY AND THE BIRTH
OF THE NEUTRAL STRIP

Concerned over the aggressive actions of the Spanish, in March 1806, the Jefferson administration directed General Wilkinson to transfer all troops from St. Louis, except for one company, to Fort Adams (located in Mississippi and about forty miles south of Natchez). Colonel T.H. Cushing was dispatched with three companies of infantry and two field artillery pieces to reinforce the two hundred soldiers at Natchitoches under Major Porter's command. Wilkinson was slow to obey the order, delaying their departure until May 6, but after the troops left St. Louis, Wilkinson received reports from Porter about the large buildup of Spanish troops in Texas and Florida. The general sent orders to Cushing to push his advance as fast as possible, and on arrival in the Orleans Territory, Cushing was to determine if the Spanish were more likely to invade from Texas or West Florida (the tip of modern Louisiana, including Baton Rouge, and the Mississippi and Alabama Gulf Coast plus the panhandle of Florida) and combine his forces with either the garrison at Fort Adams or Fort Claiborne. Cushing arrived at Natchitoches on June 1 and took command. Additional orders were sent by Jefferson's cabinet to deploy nine warships to Louisiana, to repair the fortifications of New Orleans and build new fortifications as needed and to drill the militia. Plans were prepared to seize Mobile, Pensacola and Baton Rouge in the event of war. On May 6, Wilkinson was ordered to take personal command of the situation. His orders were to repeal any invasion and to warn the governors of Texas and West Florida that the boundary lines of the Louisiana Purchase must be respected.[12] It was into one of the most volatile diplomatic and military situations in the history of the young republic that President Jefferson sent one of the least trusted public figures in the country, for James Wilkinson held many titles: commanding general of the United States Army, governor of the Louisiana Territory and Spanish Agent 13.

James Wilkinson was born in Maryland in 1757 on an almost nine-hundred-acre plantation owned by his parents, Joseph and Betty Heighe Wilkinson. His father died in 1764, leaving the seven-year-old a large inheritance. Seventeen-year-old Wilkinson was sent to Philadelphia to study medicine in 1773, the year of the Boston Tea Party, and was soon caught up in the spirit of revolution. He was in Monocacy, Maryland, working on his medical studies in 1775, so he missed the Battles of Lexington, Concord and Bunker Hill, but he quickly volunteered in a rifle regiment and joined the army forming around Boston. Wilkinson soon began his practice of befriending superior officers to speed his path up the promotion ladder. He first endeared himself to Colonels John Stark and Joseph Reed, the heroes of Bunker Hill, by asking questions of them during a tour of the battlefield that were calculated to show his interest and intelligence while at the same time stroking their egos, ensuring that the young officer would be remembered. While only eighteen, Wilkinson soon earned a position on General Greene's staff. When Greene was transferred to New York, away from Washington's headquarters, Wilkinson quickly maneuvered a transfer to Colonel Reed's staff to remain at the center of power and influence. During the war, Wilkinson would serve on the staffs of General Benedict Arnold (the most famous traitor in American history), as well as General Charles Lee and General Horatio Gates, both of whom actively conspired to replace George Washington as commanding general.[13]

Wilkinson was promoted to brigadier general after the Battle of Saratoga and was transferred to the Board of War, where he was selected as secretary. It was during this time that his continued involvement with General Gates's attempts to replace Washington as commanding general became known. He was forced to resign from the Board of War and transferred to the clothier general department, where he served from 1779 until March 1781, when he resigned due to allegations of financial misconduct. Wilkinson ended the war as a brigadier general of the Pennsylvania militia and a member of the state legislature.[14]

After the war, Wilkinson began his civilian life by settling in frontier Kentucky, but his lifestyle outpaced his income, and he soon turned to intrigue to pay his bills. In 1787, Wilkinson traveled to Spanish New

Orleans, where he negotiated a trading monopoly with the Crown but also agreed to provide information about how Spain could separate the western territories from the United States and other useful information. Now known to his Spanish handlers as Agent 13, Wilkinson would send information for many years. His income from information selling continued even after his mercantile monopoly was broken with the opening of the Mississippi River trade in 1791.[15]

In 1790, the United States suffered two of its worst defeats at the hands of Native Americans, and after the loss of those two mostly volunteer armies, it was decided that a professional army would be needed to fight the coalition of tribes under Chief Little Turtle, so the army was reorganized and trained under General "Mad" Anthony Wayne. Wilkinson received a commission as the lieutenant colonel of the Second U.S. Infantry in 1792 and fought at the Battle of Fallen Timbers in August 1794. With the sudden death of Wayne in 1796, Wilkinson was promoted to commanding general of the army with the rank of brigadier general, a post he would hold through four presidential administrations. Wilkinson was not trusted by the civilian government, and rumors of his close financial ties to the Spanish and his possible involvement as a spy would haunt him throughout his career. Yet with no proof of disloyalty and his strong support within the military, no president or secretary of war would risk trying to remove him. In fact, most in the government felt it was better to have him as commander of the army so that he could be monitored, and they felt that his ego would help prevent any type of military coup, which might endanger his status. The army was loyal to him, so if the government could keep Wilkinson loyal to them, he would keep the army loyal to the government. For the most part, this plan worked, as there were several times when disputes between the government and the army could have ended in a revolt, but Wilkinson either found a compromise or sided with the government, ending the threat. After the Louisiana Purchase, Wilkinson commanded the troops that accompanied the new governor of Orleans (modern-day Louisiana), William C.C. Claiborne, to New Orleans to oversee the transfer of the territory. After ensuring the peaceful transfer of the territory to the United States, James Wilkinson traveled to St. Louis to assume his role as governor of the Territory of Louisiana (all the territory north of the modern state of Louisiana) while maintaining his role as commanding general.[16]

Unfortunately for Wilkinson, his tenure as governor was plagued by controversy, as his political rivals brought up every scandal that the general had ever been accused of—not only the old rumors of him being a Spanish spy, but also new reports that he had been in contact with the Spanish in Mexico City since taking office. Many officials in President Jefferson's cabinet were becoming alarmed by the amount of power Wilkinson had over both military and civilian affairs, especially if the rumors of his status as a Spanish agent were true. Wilkinson's self-esteem had always been tied to the opinion he thought his superiors had of him. The thought that President Jefferson might be losing faith in him and rumors that he was to be replaced soon sent the general into a state of depression. It was at this moment that former vice president Aaron Burr entered the picture.

Aaron Burr had fought in the American Revolution, studied law, served as attorney general of New York and been elected to both the New York Assembly and the United States Senate. Burr was seen as charming and intelligent by his friends, but his enemies saw him as ambitious, manipulative and of poor moral character. In the 1800 presidential race, Burr and Thomas Jefferson tied, so the race was to be decided by the House of Representatives. Thirty-five times the House voted, and thirty-five times the vote was tied. However, on the thirty-sixth vote, one representative changed his vote, and Jefferson became president. Under the Constitution at this time, whichever candidate had the second-highest number of votes became the vice president. Burr became the vice president, but due to the slanderous nature of the election and the controversy over the House vote, there was bad blood between Jefferson and Burr that, combined with dissenting views on many issues, guaranteed trouble between the two men. But whatever issues existed between Burr and Jefferson were nothing compared to those between Burr and Alexander Hamilton. Burr was now being attacked by the supporters of both Jefferson and Hamilton. After the Constitution was changed to allow the presidential candidate to pick their own running mate, it was obvious that Jefferson would not pick Burr, so Burr decided to run for governor of New York; however, Hamilton and his supporters continued their attacks, and finally, Burr challenged Hamilton to a duel. Hamilton was killed in the duel, and with his death, Burr's chances of regaining political influence in the East were ended.[17]

However, Burr soon learned that his popularity in the West was growing—not only from the news of the duel, which was still seen as a legitimate way to solve disputes, but also because his policies were seen as being more favorable to the farmers and the frontiersmen in the Mississippi Valley than Hamilton's, which were very supportive of East Coast merchants. Burr soon started meeting with western leaders, and before long, their anger over government mistreatment turned to plotting how to separate the Ohio and Mississippi Valleys from the United States and possibly combine them with Mexico to create a western empire with Burr as the king and who else but Wilkinson as the military commander. When Burr met with Wilkinson, Burr laid on all the charm to inflate Wilkinson's ego, while at the same time playing on his fears of being replaced as governor and possibly even as commanding general.

The United States' response to the increasing numbers of Spanish troops moving into Texas was to send reinforcements to Natchitoches and to transfer the commanding general to personally command the troops in the region. This would seem like a logical order, but James Wilkinson saw his transfer from the territorial governorship of Louisiana to a field command as a demotion and an insult that took him further into Burr's conspiracy. Even though he received the order to travel to Orleans Territory as quickly as possible on May 6, it was not until September 7 that he reached Natchez. What was the cause of the delay? No one is sure, but many believe the timing is further proof of the general's role in the Burr conspiracy.[18]

After seeing to the strengthening of the forts closest to West Florida and meeting with Governor Williams and Claiborne, Wilkinson arrived in Natchitoches on September 22 and set about preparing for operations against the Spanish. The general had around twelve thousand men under his command throughout the Orleans and Mississippi Territory. Although he felt that he did not have enough ammunition, mules or tents, he reported that he was prepared to move against the Spanish with the troops and supplies on hand. Wilkinson sent a message to the new governor of Texas, Antonio Cordero, at Nacogdoches, informing him that he was to remove all Spanish troops from Bayou Pierre and all the territory east of the Sabine River. Even before the Americans began marching to the Sabine, General Nemesio Salcedo, the overall Spanish commander, ordered all the Crown's forces west of the Sabine to return to Texas. Tensions on the frontier eased, but on October 8, the general received a message that threatened not only his career but also the fate of the young United States.

That night, as the general and Colonel Cushing sat down for an evening meal, a twenty-three-year-old New Yorker arrived at Fort Claiborne. Samuel Swartwout claimed he was a volunteer who wanted to serve against the Spanish, but in fact, he was a messenger from Aaron Burr. Wilkinson and Burr had not communicated in almost two months, but now, the message Swartwout delivered shocked the general. Burr, unaware that the threat of war with Spain had diminished, announced that the final preparations were almost complete and the lead elements would begin moving downriver on

November 1. The main force would reach Natchez, Mississippi, between the fifth and fifteenth of December. Once there, Wilkinson was to decide if Baton Rouge (which was still part of Spanish Florida and not yet part of Louisiana) was to be captured or bypassed.[19]

The timing of the letter could not have been worse. Had war broken out in September, the letter would have seemed like the correspondence between the American military commander and a patriotic American offering troops to help in time of war. Now, the letter connected Wilkinson to what was, at the very least, an illegal campaign to capture another country's territory and, at worst, a plan to start a revolt against the United States. Even worse for General Wilkinson, Burr named him several times in the letter as a part of the plan and the military adviser, referring to Wilkinson as "second only to Burr" and requesting him to select officers for Burr's army.

With Burr already on the move, Wilkinson had to act fast. The general was aware that war with Spain was central to Burr's plan, and even with the easing of tensions, there were still possibilities that could start a war. In the spring of 1806, Wilkinson had sent Zebulon Pike to explore the Arkansas and Red Rivers, even though much of that territory was claimed by the Spanish. If Pike's forces were attacked or arrested, the public outcry could force Jefferson to declare war. But by the fall of 1806, there had been no word from Pike indicating any problems with the Spanish. Wilkinson's other option was to move his forces to the east bank of the Sabine; if the Spanish saw the U.S. deployment to the Sabine River as hostile and crossed the river to launch a preemptive strike against the American camp, it would certainly lead to war.

As always, Wilkinson's loyalty was to himself, and this was a situation that he could not just walk away from. Even if Wilkinson were to warn the government about Burr's plan, there was enough evidence of his involvement in the plot to end his career. If he turned on Burr, not only was he betraying a friend, but Burr could also easily implicate Wilkinson in the plot. But like any good gambler, Wilkinson must have wondered what would happen if Burr was successful. The general knew that he had more enemies than friends in the American government, and the wealth of Mexico's silver mines appealed to his high taste of living. There was also the matter of his Spanish handlers. How would they react to the news that Agent 13 had been involved in planning part of a plot to capture Mexico?

It was at this point, with the fate of two countries hanging in the balance, that Wilkinson decided to play for time. On October 22, the general sent a letter to Secretary of War Henry Dearborn outlining the possibility of an armed attack on Mexico by some disgruntled frontiersmen that would start from New Orleans—along with heavily edited versions of Burr's letters—and Wilkinson's plan to advance to the Sabine River in order to negotiate the boundary question so that he could then deploy his force to protect New Orleans. On the twenty-third, Wilkinson sent a message to Lieutenant Colonel Thomas Freeman warning him to prepare the city of New Orleans for an impending attack, without giving him any details about who would attack or where they would attack from. After sending his message to Freeman on October 23, Wilkinson set out on a forced march to the Sabine River. Once there, he sent Captain Walter Burling to contact Governor Cordero with the proposal that both sides evacuate the area between the Sabine River and the Arroyo Hondo until a formal treaty could be worked out by their governments. The boundaries of the Neutral Strip were loosely defined in this agreement, which set the western boundary at the Sabine River, but the eastern boundary would prove more difficult as farther south of the Arroyo Hondo, there was no continuous body of water. The accepted eastern boundary was a rough line from the Arroyo Hondo to Kisatchie Bayou, then through the Calcasieu River to the Gulf of Mexico. The northern boundary was the thirty-second parallel north of Natchitoches. The agreement was accepted by both sides on November 6, and Wilkinson quickly returned to Natchitoches.[20]

When he arrived in Natchitoches, Wilkinson found more letters from Burr, updating him on the conspiracy and informing him that President Jefferson was turning against the general and would soon ask for his resignation. For whatever reason—out of fear that since there would be no war with Spain to mask Burr's true plot, it would fail; fear that he would lose his Spanish pension; fear that he would lose his rank and military career; or out of a true sense of patriotism—Wilkinson decided to turn on his old friend and set off to New Orleans. Burr was eventually captured and brought to trial for treason, and who other than James Wilkinson was the star witness against him. Although the jury could not find enough evidence to convict him of treason, most of the country felt that Burr was guilty, and Wilkinson with him. Wilkinson may even have had another motive: in 1807, rumors were published in the newspapers that Wilkinson had received a very large payment from Spain for his role in stopping Burr's plot. His choice of the Sabine as the river the Americans claimed for the western side of the Neutral Strip would also weaken the United States' claim in future negotiations over the boundary and over keeping Texas as part of Spanish Mexico—for which, according to the rumors, he also received payment, or at least demanded it. But these reports were never proven. Although his reputation was tarnished, Wilkinson would retain his rank and position until 1813, when after a series of defeats in the War of 1812, he was forced to retire. He died in Mexico City in 1825.

Whether because of patriotism or his own self-interest, James Wilkinson had left the United States with a strip of land, roughly five thousand square miles, over which neither the United States nor Spain could establish law and order. As a result, the Neutral Ground quickly became a haven for outlaws, who would prey on travelers and merchants moving through No Man's Land and who would commit crimes in either Texas or the surrounding states, then flee back to the safety of the Neutral Ground, where neither U.S. nor Spanish officials could pursue them. Over the next decade and a half, the lawlessness of the region would become infamous, and while there were some legitimate settlers in the region, most of the inhabitants had less than virtuous reasons to be there.

CHAPTER 3

A LAND OF OUTLAWS, SMUGGLERS AND FILIBUSTERS

Five thousand square miles of heavily forested area with a major international highway running through the middle of it and no police or military force within thirty miles was too tempting a target. Soon, bands of robbers were roaming the woods, attacking settlers moving to Texas and merchants traveling between Natchitoches and Nacogdoches. Between 1806 and 1821, the Neutral Ground earned its nickname of Devil's Playground as flocks of outlaws and smugglers flooded into the area. There was no crime that did not take place in the Sabine Strip, and no one who entered the Neutral Ground could feel truly safe unless they had more guns and more men than the outlaws.

Even though settlement was supposed to be banned in the Neutral Strip, free land and no government attracted many settlers who could not afford the rising cost of land in the United States. These settlers, along with travelers moving along the Texas Road, made a tempting target. While some outlaws would wait in the woods to ambush travelers, many criminals learned that travelers were most vulnerable at watering holes and overnight camps, and these soon became prime targets. Many of the highwaymen's identities were never known, and some were just known by nicknames, like Uncle Blood Lewing, who roamed the area from Natchitoches through where the towns of Many and Robeline would one day be founded. According to legend, he was so successful at robbing travelers that he soon had more money than he needed, and he and his family lived off his ill-gotten loot for the rest of their lives.[21]

Both Spanish and American travelers were attacked by these roaming bands of highwaymen, some of which were very large. In 1811, Jose Zepeda and his three employees were attacked by a large band of thieves. Also in 1811, a party of seventeen Spaniards was attacked near the Sabine by thirty renegade Americans, and over thirty outlaws attacked several traders along Bayou Pierre later that year. Having an armed escort did not always help: Don de Apolinar Masmela and a detachment of eleven soldiers and fifteen settlers were attacked in 1812.[22]

Two of the major trails through the Neutral Strip were El Camino Real and Nolan's Trace. Philip Nolan is another historical figure whose life and folklore are so mixed it is hard to tell fact from fiction. What is known is that Nolan was an employee of James Wilkinson during Wilkinson's time as a merchant, before he rejoined the army, and Nolan made several trips to New Orleans for Wilkinson. At some point, Nolan and Wilkinson decided that there was a lot of money to be made trading in Spanish horses from Texas, which was banned by the Spanish government in Texas at this time. Undeterred, Wilkinson used his connections with the Spanish in Louisiana to get Nolan passports. Nolan made his first trip into Texas in 1791 and brought back a herd of beautiful wild horses, turning a nice profit for all involved. Nolan made two more trips into Texas, but by 1800, relations had broken down between the United States and Spain. Spain's belief that Nolan was really laying the groundwork for an American takeover of Texas led to Nolan and his men being ambushed near the future site of Blum, Texas, by 150 Spanish soldiers. Nolan was killed in the battle, along with several others. The survivors continued to fight after Nolan's death, but they were soon overrun and taken prisoner. Even though Nolan was killed, he proved the economic value of trading livestock, such as horses and cattle, between Louisiana and Texas, starting large-scale cattle and horse drives almost a century before the cowboy days of the late 1800s. Nolan also located several important trails that would be used to move not only livestock but also settlers into Texas.[23]

Although Nolan took a different route into Texas each time he went, the path he took on his second-to-last trip became known as Nolan's Trace. It crossed the Sabine River near the same place as the southern path of El Camino Real, then turned south, passing through what would become Sabine Parish and down to Alexandria through what would become Vernon Parish. About four miles south of where the town of Many would be founded was a popular watering hole and campsite for those traveling the Nolan Trace called Fallen Springs. Unfortunately for

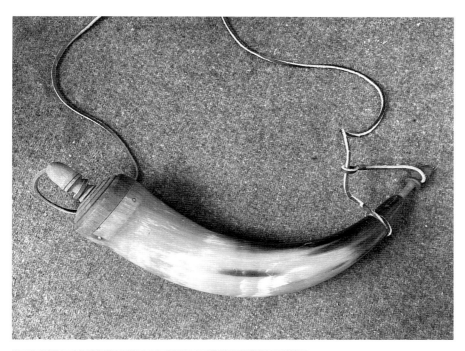

Above: All firearms in the early nineteenth century were muzzle loaders, which meant that powder had to be poured down the barrel and the bullet pushed down the barrel. It took almost a minute to reload the rifle. This is a reproduction of a typical powder horn. *Photo by author.*

Left: All shot and other shooting supplies would be carried in a shot bag—like this leather reproduction—worn over the shoulder. *Photo by author.*

the travelers, outlaws also knew the popularity of the spot and preyed on those who stopped there to rest or spend the night, robbing the travelers and sometimes murdering them to cover the outlaws' presence.[24]

One story that has been handed down involves a group of men bringing mules from Texas to trade at Natchitoches. The owner of the mule train rode ahead of the group to scout the path. Not long after crossing the Sabine River, he was ambushed by highwaymen planning to steal the mules. The owner was given the option of being murdered or fleeing the area without warning the rest of the group. The owner acted like he was scared for his life and fled into the woods, but he soon circled back to follow the thieves and warn his men. When the thieves attacked, a gunfight ensued; several of the thieves were killed, and the rest fled. The mule train crossed the rest of the Neutral Strip without incident.[25]

Most of the Spanish trade between Nacogdoches and Natchitoches was conducted by the trading house of Davenport and Barr (founded in 1798), which would purchase merchandise and goods in Natchitoches and transport them to Texas to trade with local tribes and settlers in Nacogdoches for furs, pelts and horses, then transport those back to Louisiana to trade for more goods. Davenport and Barr also helped to provide the garrison at Nacogdoches with supplies and the tribes with gifts of trade goods on behalf of the government of New Spain. His convoys were attacked so often that by 1812, he had reported to the Spanish government, "The Neutral Ground is still infested by gangs of bandits, and it is impossible to carry on business. I dare not risk my interests to capture by outlaws." With President Jefferson's 1807 Embargo Act severely limiting the legal trade between Natchitoches and Nacogdoches, smuggling of goods became a highly profitable business—but brought even more violence to No Man's Land.[26]

One of the early smugglers to use the region of No Man's Land was Jean Lafitte. Jean was born in 1776, and he and his brother Pierre became famous as smugglers after the Louisiana Purchase by supplying the French and Spanish citizens of New Orleans with French goods, whose importation was either banned by the U.S. government or deemed too expensive when U.S. import taxes were added to the price. He quickly became a hero to the Creole population, as the European residents saw him as standing up to American trade laws, which the Creoles felt unjustly favored new American settlers at the expense of the former residents. With the passing of the Embargo Act in 1807, Lafitte's operations increased. The Embargo Act was President Jefferson's attempt to keep America neutral during the Napoleonic wars by saying that America would not trade with either France or Great Britain or with any other nation at war.[27]

The Embargo Act may have been Jefferson's attempt to keep America neutral, but all it would do was destroy the U.S. economy, anger the New England states and the Creoles in Louisiana and lead to widespread smuggling. The Lafitte brothers took full advantage of the anger over the act and the location of the Neutral Strip. Before 1815, their headquarters was an area of swamp near New Orleans known as Barataria, and Pierre's blacksmith shop in New Orleans was their primary meeting place and trade center. However, the area between the Sabine and the Calcasieu Rivers also proved useful as not only a hiding area, since neither Spanish or American ships could follow Jean there, but also a source of food and other supplies, which Jean would trade with farmers along the two rivers. It has been said that after the Embargo Act, the Lafittes made more money from captured manufactured goods than they did from the gold and silver they looted from the ships they raided. In 1814–15, when the British attempted to invade New Orleans, the Lafittes provided gunpowder, shot, cannons and men who knew how to use them to the American military. Although they probably were not present during the battle, their support and the arms and men they provided helped Andrew Jackson stop the British invasion. Although seen as heroes and given pardons, the Lafittes soon ran afoul of the American authorities again and were chased out of New Orleans. They established their new headquarters on Galveston Island and expanded their operations in the Neutral Strip. Soon, they would have new schemes and new partners.[28]

With the outlawing of the importation of slaves into the United States in 1808, slave smuggling was added to the list of activities in No Man's Land. Jean Lafitte, Jim Bowie and dozens of others used the lawless region as a base for their operations. Lafitte soon figured out that he could make a fortune not by smuggling slaves himself but by establishing a marketplace for others to come and purchase illegal slaves. People would travel to Lafitte's base at Galveston, purchase the slaves, then slip up the Sabine or Calcasieu River and travel overland to Opelousas, Alexandria or Natchitoches to sell them. Jim Bowie and his brother developed a unique way to double their profits. They would purchase contraband slaves from Jean Lafitte and other smugglers, transport them through the Neutral Ground, then claim they had recovered the slaves as runaways. When the smuggled slaves were sold at auction, a reward of half the sale price was given to the Bowies. To make even more money, the Bowie brothers would have agents purchase the smuggled slaves at the auction, then resell them a few weeks later. This way, the Bowies were able to collect not only the reward but also the sales price of the smuggled slaves. It is estimated that the Bowie brothers averaged a 40 to 60 percent return on their investment through this scheme.[29]

Some of the outlaws used their entrepreneurial skills to set up inns and taverns along the Texas Road and other trails, but these were opened not out of a sense of hospitality but to make it easier to rob and cheat. One of these inns was known as the Twenty-Five Mile House or Halfway House and was opened around 1813 by Peter Parker and his four brothers, about a mile from where Fort Jesup would be established. The Parkers were smart enough to not steal from every customer but wait for the right opportunities. Although the Parkers do not appear to have been as bloodthirsty as some of the other No Man's Land gangs, that doesn't mean that the Parkers did not commit murder—however, they do seem to have been more calculating in their use of murder, only turning to murder to cover their tracks. To aid in their endeavors, they employed several craftsmen, including a blacksmith named William Black, who was an expert at disguising stolen knives, guns, watches and other metal items. Another craftsman in their employ was Henry Tully, whose skill was disguising saddles and other leather items. Slave smuggling was also part of the Parkers' enterprise. The Parkers and Henry Tully would purchase slaves from Jean Lafitte, bring them across No Man's Land, then sell them. Often, the Parkers would use one of their slaves to act as a Judas—someone who would move from plantation to plantation along the Red River encouraging slaves to escape to the Neutral Strip, where the Parkers and their gang were waiting. Instead of their freedom, the runaways found the Parkers, who would either sell them at auction or return them for a reward. Eventually, the Parkers decided they had made enough money and turned away from criminal activity. After a time, they burned down the Halfway House so no other criminals could use it and took their possessions to Texas to start a new life.[30]

Counterfeiting was also a popular activity in No Man's Land, as the Neutral Strip provided a convenient hiding place to produce the fake money. Paper money was not very common in the U.S. economy at this time, and most money in circulation was coinage. Because few silver coins could be produced by U.S. mints, due to a lack of silver mines in the United States at the time, Spanish silver dollars were considered legal tender. This was convenient for those conducting business in the Neutral Strip, as countries on both sides of the strip used the same silver dollar, but it was even more convenient for counterfeiters, as it doubled the opportunities to pass their counterfeit coins. One traveler through No Man's Land met

Reproduction Spanish silver piece of eight on display at Fort Jesup State Historic Site. Often, these coins would be cut into smaller pieces or "bits" to pay for items that cost less than a dollar. *Photo by author.*

one of the counterfeiters and recorded his story in his diary. Luckily for the traveler but unluckily for us, when the diary was published, the name of the counterfeiter was changed to John Doe, since he was still alive at the time the journal was published. According to the account, John Doe would use a copper core wrapped with a silver lining—and sometimes, the lining came off. Apparently, one day, an area Indian brought Doe a coin that had lost its lining. Doe calmly explained to the Indian that coins, like snakes, shed their skin and gave him a new coin. According to the stories, Doe, like so many other counterfeiters before and since, got overconfident and was discovered by American authorities on a trip outside of the Neutral Strip. He was arrested and sent to prison.[31]

Although soldiers from either Spain or the United States were not supposed to enter the strip, outlaw activity became so rampant that in 1810, the governor of Spanish Texas, Manuel Salcedo, suggested that a joint expedition be launched to clear the strip of outlaws and illegal settlers. The American secretary of war, William Eustis, approved the suggestion, and on August 1, the American and Spanish troops met at La Piedra, west of the Arroyo Hondo. The American detachment from Fort Claiborne was made up of one sergeant, one corporal and fifteen privates, under the command of Lieutenant William Magee. The Spanish had an equal number of soldiers, under the command of Lieutenant Don Jose Maria Guadiana. For the next twelve days, the force traveled the Neutral Strip, driving out thirty-four intruders and burning twelve houses. The persons evicted were allowed to remove their furniture, cattle and corn.[32]

In 1812, a second expedition was sent into the Neutral Strip, because the number of robbers and highwaymen preying on merchants and other travelers had increased to the point that trade almost stopped completely along El Camino Real. The Spanish first suggested this expedition in July 1811, but it took the Americans until February 1812 to send Lieutenant Colonel Zebulon Pike from Baton Rouge to Fort Claiborne to oversee the operation. Pike sent a letter to the Spanish inviting them to participate in the expedition, but he started (and completed) the operation before the Spanish had time to respond. Pike sent Lieutenant Augustus Magee with two subalterns and fifty men into the Neutral Strip with orders to remove all intruders who had settled there after 1806 and to burn their houses and improvements. A civilian law enforcement officer accompanied the party to arrest anyone suspected of murder or robbery. The detachment left Fort Claiborne on March 4 and returned on March 17. During their time in No Man's Land, they arrested thirteen men suspected of robbery, burned nine houses belonging to both Spanish and American settlers and recovered thirty stolen horses and mules, sixteen guns, ammunition and other merchandise. Since Natchitoches did not yet have a civilian jail, the accused were kept in the Fort Claiborne guardhouse until one could be built. The thirteen men were eventually taken to Rapides Parish and tried by the superior court there. Two were found guilty of robbery and sentenced to seven years of hard labor. The others were acquitted. The success of these expeditions is questionable, because after each expedition, the illegal settlers and criminals moved back into the strip as soon as the soldiers left. There would be no more formal expeditions into No Man's Land, as the War of 1812 stretched the resources of the young American republic to its limits and Spain was involved in both the Mexican Revolution and the Napoleonic Wars. However, after 1812, soldiers from Fort Claiborne were allowed to escort caravans of money or goods through No Man's Land at the request of merchants, if the merchants were willing to provide horses for the troops.[33]

Another illegal activity that the Neutral Strip would become famous for was filibustering. The modern term refers to delaying a vote in the Senate through extended debate and speechmaking, but in the nineteenth century, it referred to a military invasion by private citizens of a foreign country that the United States was at peace with. The term came from the Dutch term *vrijbuiter* ("freebooter"), which meant "land pirate" or "thief." When the Mexican Revolution began in 1810, many in the United States were sympathetic toward the Mexican revolutionaries, seeing them as fellow freedom fighters, as their own fathers had been against the British. But there

Top: Reproduction of an 1803 U.S. rifle. *Photo by author.*

Bottom: Reproduction of a U.S. infantry officer's eagle head saber. This style of saber was used from the early 1800s to the 1830s. *Photo by author.*

were also those who saw the revolution as a chance to acquire cheap land in Texas by separating it from Mexico and either creating an independent country or joining it with the United States (which still claimed that Texas was part of the Louisiana Purchase). Although this was not officially supported by the American government, it did little to stop these expeditions, either. The United States was unwilling to start a war with an ally of Napoleon at the same time it was facing a war with Great Britain and a possible Indian War around the Great Lakes, but the idea of an independent Mexico was supported by most Americans.[34]

The confused nature of the American position toward the Mexican Revolution would lead to even more confusion within the American military. New Orleans and Natchitoches were open recruiting and supply bases for the filibusters, but the military had no orders to stop them from assembling or stockpiling weapons. On the few occasions when civilian law enforcement arrested a suspected filibuster, the case was often thrown out for lack of evidence. It soon became the position of the commander at Fort Claiborne that the military was only to become involved in stopping the filibusters if civilian law enforcement called on them for assistance. Since most of those in civilian law enforcement supported the filibusters, this created a convenient loophole. To further confuse the issue, the filibusters would not meet in armed bands or units within Natchitoches or U.S. territory, instead waiting until they reached the Neutral Strip, which was outside of the jurisdiction of both the military and law enforcement. In 1812, General Wilkinson requested from the War Department that soldiers be allowed to patrol the area around the Sabine to stop illegal filibuster activity, but the secretary of war still limited the army's activities to the east side of the Arroyo Hondo, just outside of the Neutral Strip.[35]

The first major filibuster was led by José Bernardo Gutiérrez, an exile from Spanish Mexico who began to gather men and supplies at Natchitoches in April 1812. In fact, Gutiérrez was entertained at Fort Claiborne for several days by the post commander, Captain Overton, who also threw a banquet in his honor. While Gutiérrez was at the fort, both Captain Overton and Dr. John Sibley coached Gutiérrez "in the language of American republicanism, and gave him letters of introduction to the Secretary of War and other officials and important people living along the road from Natchitoches to Washington D.C." In fact, the only attempt that Overton would make to stop any part of the Gutiérrez filibuster was in October 1812, when Overton marched his command to the community of Bayou Pierre, where there were reports that Gutiérrez was forcing members of the community to join his army. Overton disbursed the filibusters, and he assured the community that they lived in the jurisdiction of the United States and that no one could force them to join a filibuster against their will.[36]

The Gutiérrez expedition numbered around 130 men, including William Shaler as an official U.S. government observer and a former officer from Fort Claiborne, Augustus William Magee, who had resigned his commission to join the revolutionaries. In the summer of 1812, the expedition traveled through the Neutral Strip, crossed the Sabine River and occupied Nacogdoches. As word spread of their success, Gutiérrez's force soon swelled to around six hundred men, as more American volunteers from Louisiana and Arkansas joined the "Republican Army of the North."

Although the Madison administration sent a representative to the government of New Spain to voice America's disapproval of the border violation, there was little the United States could have done to stop it even had it wanted to, as America was preparing for the War of 1812 and all military resources were being sent to the Canadian border, further reducing the already small garrison at Fort Claiborne. Although the U.S. observer William Shaler remained with the expedition for over a year, he was officially recalled on June 5, 1813. After defeating the royalist forces, Gutiérrez began losing men and support when he ordered the execution of the Spanish governor and his aides. Magee had died of unknown causes, though some thought he was poisoned, soon after the taking of La Bahia (known as Goliad today). Two months later, on August 18, 1813, a royalist army defeated what was left of the republican army at the Battle of Medina and marched to retake Nacogdoches. Ahead of this army were over one thousand refugees and survivors of the republican army, who flooded into the Neutral Ground and the safety of the Sabine River. The Spanish army left a trail of abandoned farms and burned buildings, as both revolutionaries and peaceful settlers fled for fear of retaliation. East Texas was almost totally depopulated, leaving a desolate, empty land.[37]

Had the Spanish wanted it to, the five-thousand-man army they sent into East Texas could have easily crossed the Sabine, wiped out Fort Claiborne and marched through North Louisiana to join with the much larger Spanish army at Mobile, then turned south to take New Orleans, which many in the U.S. military feared was about to happen. However, logistical difficulties prevented the Spanish from crossing the Sabine for a punitive raid on the United States or even to chase the escaping filibusters. Unlike during the 1806 border crisis, by 1813, Spain could not support a large army in East Texas, and not long after taking Nacogdoches, the Spanish returned to the interior of Mexico.[38]

In 1815, Captain Perry, who had been a follower of Magee, attempted to raise an army in New Orléans to invade Texas. President Madison came out strongly against this, issuing a proclamation and ordering authorities to stop this and any other future filibusters. Perry was able to raise a small band of troops and evaded authorities long enough to cross the Sabine. By 1816, they had reached Galveston Island to join the revolutionaries Herrera and Avery. Dozens of ships were sent out as privateers under the flag of revolution. However, disagreements between Herrera and Avery soon split the army, as Herrera wanted to invade Mexico and Avery wanted to operate only in Texas. Both Avery and Perry abandoned the expedition; Avery returned to Galveston, but Perry's force was ambushed and annihilated. Avery soon left Galveston to join forces with another filibuster, Gregor MacGregor, and not long after Avery's forces left, Jean Lafitte moved in to establish his base of operations on the island.[39]

The 1815 proclamation banning all filibustering activity originating on U.S. soil included orders to the U.S. Army to stop any attempt to organize or launch filibusters by American citizens. General Andrew Jackson—who had been given command of the southern military district after the War of 1812, during which he successfully defended New Orleans from the British—was aware that the small garrison of Fort Claiborne was unable to do anything to stop the filibusters, but he would have to wait several months before he could transfer more troops to the Spanish border. Near the end of 1815, Jackson ordered two companies from the U.S. Rifle Regiment sent to reinforce the garrison, and two additional companies of the First U.S. Infantry were sent at the beginning of 1816. These additional troops allowed the garrison of Fort Claiborne to conduct patrols and sweeps through the middle and upper part of the Neutral Ground in 1816 and 1817, but to little effect. Military leaders in Louisiana pushed for a permanent post in the Neutral Ground, which could be an effective deterrent to the filibusters who used it as a staging area, but until the boundary question was officially settled, the War Department was unwilling to build any type of permanent garrison in No Man's Land.[40]

In mid-1818, word reached Fort Claiborne that another Spanish army was marching toward the Sabine River, this time in response to the Mina Expedition, which had, a few weeks earlier, assembled in the Neutral Strip and crossed the Sabine. The expedition had captured La Bahia and was creating a flood of revolutionary activity, as many residents of the southern United States were ready to take up arms and go to Nacogdoches to assist the rebellion. General Eleazer W. Ripley, commander of the Eighth Military District, ordered three more companies of the First Infantry to reinforce Fort Claiborne. One company was left to guard Fort Claiborne, and all the other companies were spread out at key crossings of the Red River to block Americans from going to Texas and the Spanish from pursuing survivors of the expedition into Louisiana. As with all the previous filibusters, the Mina Expedition was soon defeated by the Spanish. However, this time, the survivors would be saved not by the U.S. Army but by Mother Nature. A massive hurricane blew inland from the Gulf of Mexico, dumping heavy rains on the province and making travel for the Spanish army almost impossible. The Spanish were unable to move much farther east than San Antonio, allowing the survivors to escape to the safety of No Man's Land. On learning that the Spanish army was heading back to Mexico, General Ripley recalled all six of the First Infantry companies spread out along the Red River to Fort Claiborne.[41]

Starting in 1817, negotiations between Secretary of State John Quincy Adams and Spanish minister Luis de Onís began to determine where the western boundary would be. On February 22, 1819, a treaty titled the

Transcontinental Agreement (and referred to as the Adams-Onís Treaty) was signed. The document transferred all of Florida to the United States and set the boundary of Louisiana at the Sabine River; in exchange, Spain received undisputed possession of Texas. Ratification of the treaty would be delayed for two years, until 1821, by both the U.S. Senate and King Ferdinand VII of Spain, as the legal status of recent land grants was determined.[42]

The Transcontinental Agreement was not popular with all Americans, especially those in Louisiana, Mississippi and Arkansas, who felt Adams had betrayed them by giving up all claims to Texas that President Jefferson had outlined during his time in office. It was more than simple patriotism; the United States was in the grip of the economic depression of 1819, which had cost many small farmers and shopkeepers their homes and farms, and the prospect of cheap land in Texas was attractive to them. The treaty was also unpopular with many of the Spaniards living in No Man's Land, as it meant they would never be Spanish subjects again. General Ripley, commanding the Eighth Military District, was afraid that Spanish settlers unhappy with the new treaty would incite the tribes living in Texas to cross the Sabine River and attack American settlers between the river and Natchitoches. The Adams-Onís Treaty also placed No Man's Land in limbo for three years, as it was not ratified by Spain or the United States until 1821. Ripley's orders to establish a camp violated the treaty, since the land was not yet officially part of the United States.

The camp was located near Crow's Ferry, about a quarter mile south of the Natchitoches to Nacogdoches Road, and named in honor of Brigadier General E.W. Ripley, who was a hero of the War of 1812 and later became a U.S. congressman from Louisiana. Although officially known as Camp Ripley, the position was often referred to as Camp Sabine, even in official records. The garrison consisted of troops from the First Regiment of Infantry and the United States Rifle Regiment and varied in size from a company to several companies from each regiment. The average strength of the camp was normally less than one hundred men. The soldiers lived in tents at first, but soon, huts were built to house them.[43]

The Spanish never rose up against the treaty, but a group of Americans would. Not long after the details of the Adams-Onís Treaty became public, a mass meeting was held in Natchez, Mississippi, and soon, a filibustering expedition was organized to invade Texas and annex it into the United States. The expedition was led by James Long of Natchez, Mississippi, who had made several land deals in Texas, believing that the territory would soon be added to the United States as part of the negotiations. When the boundary was set at the Sabine River, his real estate deals all fell through, leaving him almost bankrupt.

The filibusters set out for Texas, with the advance party moving through Natchitoches in April or May and the main body of between 75 to 120 men passing through and around Natchitoches, crossing the Sabine River in June 1819. John Jamison, commander at Fort Claiborne, described the Long expedition as "a desperate group of vagabonds, ill-fed and clothed with Bankrupters at the head and vagabonds at the feet"; despite their patriotic sentiments, their main interest was in "Texas plunder."[44] One supporter of Long's army was General Ripley, who had resigned from the U.S. Army in 1818 under suspicious circumstances. Long apparently offered Ripley the presidency of the new country and asked him to lead the army as its general, as well as a salary of $25,000 a year and a land grant of 20 square miles, to be divided into strips of 1,280 acres each. The general wrote that he looked forward to joining in freeing Texas from the "despotic and intolerant colonial system of Spain," as well as freeing the "natural resources"[45] of Texas; however, personal issues prevented him from joining the army in the field.

General Daniel Bissell, the officer who succeeded Ripley as the department commander of the Eighth Military District, ordered Captain Robert L. Combs and a small detachment of U.S. regulars to Crow's Ferry near the east bank of the Sabine River, with instructions to observe the men gathering in the region and to stop them if they tried to cross the river. Combs was also instructed to select a site to house troops in case a permanent garrison was needed. Captain William Beard, who was in command of Fort Claiborne, requested the aid of the U.S. marshal in apprehending those men who were trying to arm themselves, but the marshal refused to act until he received orders from the United States District Court. The troops at Fort Claiborne did not stop Long, on the grounds that the filibusters had passed so far below Natchitoches that they were out of their jurisdiction. One observer commented that both the civilian and military authorities "were inclined (more) to favor than to obstruct the invasion."[46]

The *Albany Gazette* reprinted a *Louisiana Gazette* article reporting that there were so many people flocking to Long's banner that during the summer of 1819, a riverboat that had left Alexandria passed four large river barges of eighteen oars each headed toward Natchitoches—which, based on their behavior (not stopping in the town and trying to avoid observation), led the captain of the steamboat *New Port* to believe they were headed to join the filibuster. In the town of Alexandria, "the expedition was much talked of, and many proposed joining the enterprise. The first place of rendezvous is said to be fixed at thirty miles beyond the Sabine."[47]

Long's army continued to grow, recruiting more men in the Neutral Strip and East Texas, and after growing to roughly 300 men, soon captured Nacogdoches. The Spanish response was swift, and by September, around 650 soldiers were marching toward East Texas. The "Independence Army" was defeated in October, and soon, another wave of refugees was heading to the Sabine River. Unlike before, the Spanish army pursued the defeated force all the way to the Sabine River and might have even crossed the river were it not for the presence of U.S. troops encamped nearby.

Once again, the Spanish army and the United States Army were facing each other across the Sabine River. After a tense thirty minutes, negotiations began to secure the release of several Americans captured along the way to the Sabine. In exchange for their release, the American commander promised to keep Long and his men in Louisiana. However, Long and many of his followers never crossed back into Louisiana; they remained in Texas and tried to rebuild Long's army. Long launched a second expedition in 1821, not long after Mexico won its independence from Spain. Long's new army was soon forced to surrender, and the survivors were sent to Mexico City, where Long was killed by a Mexican soldier who claimed he tried to escape.[48]

After Long's first defeat, U.S. troops would remain stationed on the Sabine River until the Transcontinental Treaty could be finalized. While there, they received a visit from a young American who one day would be called the "Father of Texas." Stephen F. Austin was a guest at Camp Ripley for a few days around July 10, 1820. Stephen's father had been a successful businessman, owning several lead mines in Spanish Missouri before the Louisiana Purchase. Because of several factors beyond his control, such as U.S. trade policy, Moses Austin was soon forced to declare bankruptcy. To regain his fortune, Moses came up with a plan to bring American settlers into Spanish Texas; however, soon after getting the plan approved, Moses became ill, and his wish was for his son Austin to continue his plan. Stephen soon set off for Texas, knowing that his father would probably not survive long enough for him to return. Stephen traveled from Little Rock to Natchitoches, then to Texas. It was at Camp Ripley that Stephen received word that his father had died. Stephen stayed at the camp for a day or two, waiting on several papers and letters that were to be forwarded to him. Fearing the letters were lost, Stephen returned to Natchitoches, only to find out they had already been sent with a Spaniard, Don Erasmo, whom Stephen met along

El Camino Real on July 14. Stephen stayed at Camp Ripley on the evening of July 15, and on July 16, he entered Texas for the first time.[49]

Even with American troops on the Sabine, outlaws were still active in No Man's Land, especially smugglers of slaves and those trading alcohol and other illegal items to Native Americans, as Lieutenant Wash reported in a letter written in 1820 from Camp Sabine: "The laws of the United States relative to the introduction of slaves and to trading with the Indians are set at perfect contempt and daily and exhaustively violated."[50] While outlaws would continue to operate in the Neutral Strip for many years, the days of their impunity would soon come to an end, as the boundary of the United States and Mexico was officially set at the Sabine River in 1821. The federal government would soon be sending law enforcement officials into the region, and a large military post would be established in the center of No Man's Land to help bring law and order. Although the outlaws get most of the attention during the era of the Neutral Ground, it would be the settlers who braved the lawlessness of No Man's Land who would prove that the region truly was a land of opportunity.

CHAPTER 4

A LAND OF OPPORTUNITY

The term "No Man's Land" brings to mind a lawless region full of outlaws waiting to pounce on unwary travelers. But while there were many thieves, smugglers and murderers in the region, there were also many settlers who were willing to brave the dangers for the opportunities the region held. Some came for the land, some to trade; some planned to go to Texas but decided at the last minute not to cross the Sabine; and some wanted to escape family or legal trouble. Whatever the reason, a stream of settlers moved into No Man's Land between 1806 and 1821, with even more coming after the region officially became part of the United States in 1821. These new settlers joined the Spanish and the French, who had been in the area for around a century, and Native Americans who had been there for thousands of years. The interactions between these cultures, the region's status as a border area, the need to rely on relatives and neighbors and a distrust of outsiders would create a culture different from that of the rest of Louisiana.

Many of the early Anglo settlers who came to western Louisiana after the Louisiana Purchase were from Tennessee, Kentucky, Mississippi and Arkansas. When they arrived, they found a land similar to what they were used to back home. The upper part of the strip was hilly, with rich timberland full of loblolly, longleaf and shortleaf pine, red and white oak, black gum and dogwoods along with large cypress trees that lined the banks of the rivers. In the southern part of the strip, closer to the Gulf Coast, the land became flatter, with large areas of level ground bounded by marshes, which also provided rich timberland. Although fresh water was abundant, the soil in most of the strip was not suitable for large-scale plantation-style agriculture, which in some ways is what made the area appealing for the early settlers, as the large plantation owners had already claimed much of the best lands in their home regions, making it hard for a small farmer to make a living on the marginal, leftover lands. It was the lack of affordable land that would start waves of migration to open lands on the frontier. While the land and life were tough, the region of the Neutral Strip was well suited to small-scale farming (known as subsistence farming), supplemented with free-range hog and cattle raising (allowing the animals to graze and fatten up in the woods, which did not require large grass pastures, hay or fenced-in lands), hunting and fishing. Forests provided ample resources for building homes and making furniture, fence materials and even bowls and plates. Over the next hundred years, as more and more technology was brought into No Man's Land, the woods provided more and more income for the settlers. The region's forest industry started with settlers making shingles and fence rails by hand to sell to neighbors, and by the twentieth century, many were making crossties to sell to railroads and running their own small-scale lumber mills for cash. Those close to the rivers would often operate ferries across them or floated rafts of logs downriver to the larger sawmills.[51]

Even before the first Europeans arrived in No Man's Land, the area had been disputed between Native American tribes. By the 1700s, the northern section of the region was occupied by tribes of the Caddo Confederacy and the southern region was occupied by the Atakapa, with only limited settlement in the middle, as these two cultural groups avoided each other. Over time, other Native American groups would move into No Man's Land for a variety of reasons. Descendants of these Native people still live in No Man's Land and have added to the cultural development of the region.

The Atakapa were a small but feared tribe whose name was a Choctaw or Mobilian word meaning "eater of human flesh." The Atakapa's reputation as cannibals is questioned by some historians and anthropologists; others believe that if the Atakapa did partake in cannibalism, it was limited to eating portions of slain enemies. Most believe that their reputation for cannibalism was a way to create fear in larger tribes, since the Atakapa had only a small number of warriors. The Atakapa were secretive, rarely seen outside of swamps except during the summer months, when they fished and gathered shellfish and other seafood along the Gulf Coast. Their diet was based on fish and other animals that they hunted in the swamps and along the Gulf Coast. Their territory was from Bayou Teche to the Sabine River and from the Gulf of Mexico to modern Alexandria. Never a large tribe, their ranks thinned rapidly with the arrival of European diseases. According to one early anthropologist, there were roughly 3,500 Atakapa in 1698 and only 175 in Louisiana in 1805. By 1908, there were only nine known living descendants.[52]

Unlike the Atakapa, the Caddo were a much larger tribe with a rich material culture heritage who were willing to trade and have contact with other Native tribes and Europeans. The Caddo had a roughly thousand-year history and a territory throughout northwestern Louisiana, southern Arkansas, eastern Oklahoma and eastern Texas before the first Europeans arrived. The Caddo were seminomadic farmers who lived in villages along the river during the growing season and then made seasonal trips to their hunting grounds. By the 1700s, the Caddo had branched off into several groups that, while connected culturally and linguistically, had developed enough cultural differences to be considered different groups. The Louisiana Caddoan-speaking groups were the Adaes, Doustioni, Natchitoches, Ouachita and Yatasi, located around Natchitoches, Mansfield, Monroe and Robeline. Their territory stretched from the Ouachita River west to the Sabine River and south to the mouth of Cane River. While the Caddo did take part in intertribal warfare, they did not fight with the Europeans or, later, the Americans.[53]

By the time of the Louisiana Purchase, the Caddo population had decreased to around four hundred, of which only about one hundred were warriors. Despite the tribe's small size, it still held great influence with other tribes of the Southwest. The Caddo came into contact with Europeans early in the eighteenth century, and due to their location between the French and Spanish colonial powers, the Caddo quickly learned how to use the international competition between these powers to their advantage, not only trading with both powers for different goods but also never fully allying with either. This ensured that both powers would provide trade goods and gifts, trying to earn the Caddos' loyalty. Despite their attempts the Spanish always felt that if war broke out between Spain and France, the Caddo would side with the French, because unlike the Spanish, who had restrictive trade laws, the French not only traded more freely (including firearms and alcohol) but also were more open to cultural exchange and marriage into the tribe. Once France sold Louisiana to the United States, the Caddo attempted to continue their balancing act, appearing to grow closer to the Spanish to force the Americans into more favorable trade relations.[54]

By the early 1800s, the Caddo had moved farther north, to the area of Caddo Lake, a large body of water in the northern part of Louisiana. Their territory included land in northern Louisiana, eastern Texas and southeastern Oklahoma. The Caddo still maintained their seminomadic lifestyle, spending the spring and summer tending gardens and preparing for their fall hunt. During the fall, they crossed into Spanish Texas to the plains to hunt. It was during their fall hunts that Spanish agents would attempt to earn their loyalty, although, as before, the Caddo never fully allied themselves with either side.[55] The Caddo sold their lands in Louisiana in 1835, allowing for the settlement of Shreveport and much of northwest Louisiana. While most of the Caddo would eventually move to Oklahoma, some did not leave Louisiana in the 1830s, and some returned to the region over time. Many residents of No Man's Land have Caddo ancestors, and the Adaes Caddo still have a presence in the Spanish Lake Community.[56]

Another group to take advantage of the region was the Koasati (Coushatta). Even as early as the 1780s, Spain saw the United States' expansion as a threat to Texas and Mexico and invited the Coushatta to settle in Louisiana to act as a buffer. In the isolated area of No Man's Land, they were able to preserve much of their culture, traditional arts and ancestral language (which is still spoken by many modern tribal members). The Coushatta pine needle basket is an example of the tribe's close relationship with nature and ability to employ the available natural resources for survival. Today, most of the Coushatta are concentrated in Allen Parish, north of Elton and east of Kinder.[57]

The Choctaw Apache Tribe is a combination of several distinct tribal groups who came together in the 1700s and 1800s. After the Louisiana Purchase, groups of Choctaw began moving into West Louisiana/East Texas in search of new hunting grounds. Additional Choctaw were encouraged to move into the Neutral Strip by U.S. Indian agent John Sibley, who sought to protect them from their competing Creek and Chickasaw neighbors. Over time, they intermarried with descendants of the Spanish settlers in the Ebarb area, who themselves were descendants of Spaniards, Caddo and Lipan Apache.[58]

When most people think of Louisiana, they think of the French culture; they do not realize that several parts of the state were never settled by the French but were, instead, always Spanish. No Man's Land was one of these sections. When these American pioneers arrived, they found many areas of the Neutral Strip already occupied by Spanish settlers. The region had been settled by the Spanish in the early 1700s, and while there were a few French settlers (mostly traders or those who had married into Spanish families), the region was never part of French Louisiana, a fact that would deeply affect the cultural development of the region. When Los Adaes (originally the capital of Texas and located near modern Robeline) closed in 1773, the Spanish residents were ordered to move to San Antonio. A few took to the woods to avoid the forced exile, but most of Adaesaños endured the hardships of the march to San Antonio. Arriving at San Antonio, the Adaesaños found living conditions very difficult, and they soon petitioned the governor to allow them to return to East Texas. Many of the Adaesaños traveled to East Texas and established Nacogdoches. Still others returned to areas across the Sabine River in what would become the Neutral Strip. The early Spanish settlement would have a lasting impact on the development of No Man's Land, especially in communities such as Ebarb and Zwolle in Sabine Parish and Spanish Lake in Natchitoches Parish. Patches of Spanish settlers would dot the landscape throughout No Man's Land. Several Spanish settlers complained of ill treatment by Magee's 1812 expedition into the Neutral Strip, including Pablo Lafitte, Belun Buelier and an unnamed woman who told Spanish officer Isidro de la Garza, when he was staying in the home of Miguel Crow, about her husband being arrested by the Americans.[59]

In the 1780s and 1790s, the Spanish began giving large land grants in the area between the Arroyo Hondo and the Sabine River, which was considered part of Spanish Texas. While most of these grants were given to Spanish subjects, a few were given to Americans who had moved into the region. The first documented American merchant in the Alexandria region was Edward Murphy, who opened a store at the confluence of the Red River and Bayou Rapides at some point before 1790. Soon, Murphy joined merchants Luther Smith, William Barr and Peter Davenport to start the firm Barr and Davenport. The House of Barr and Davenport had its headquarters in Nacogdoches and supplied both the Spanish settlers and military with goods and supplies, often keeping the soldiers from starving. Because of their service, the members of the firm were given large land grants in East Texas (which at this time still included western Louisiana). Known as the LaNana Grant and located between the Sabine River and the Arroyo Hondo, this grant of twelve square miles (7,680 acres) was given to Ed Murphy in 1797. A little over forty years later, the town of Many in Sabine Parish would be founded on land that had been part of this grant. In July 1805, Murphy, Barr, Davenport and Smith bought the grant known as Los Omegas from Jacinto Mora, who had been given the 207,360 acres on November 14, 1795. The grant was located twenty-five miles from Nacogdoches on the east side of the Sabine and included land in modern Sabine and DeSoto Parishes. José M. Mora was given one square league of land about forty miles west of Natchitoches, known as La Cabeza del Nombre de Dios. Another large grant was Los Tres Llanos, given to the Sanchez family by Governor Francisco García Larios sometime between 1744 and 1748. The grant was acquired by Louis Latham sometime before 1820. Sanchez's son testified in 1820, at the age of eighty-nine years old, to Latham's legal claim to the land.[60]

The first major land grant in what would become Vernon Parish was one square league (roughly 4,439 acres) on the Anacoco Prairie, given to Juan Baptiste D'Artigeau by Antonio Gil Ybarbo, who by this time was the Spanish commandant at Nacogdoches. Other early Spanish settlers in this area were John Baptiste and Ambroise Lecomtes. While Spanish Louisiana was more open to American trade and settlement due to the Mississippi River and the port of New Orleans, great lengths were taken to prevent Americans from entering and settling in Spanish Texas. A detachment of soldiers was permanently stationed at Nacogdoches to expel Americans who did not have proper passports. While a few Americans, such as Barr and Davenport, were allowed to trade and set up operations, they also became Spanish subjects, giving up their American citizenship, and served the purposes of the Spanish Crown. Because the road from Alexandria to Nacogdoches ran through Ambroise Lecomte's land, part of the provision of the grant was that he was to arrest anyone passing through his land toward Texas without a proper Spanish passport.[61]

A new wave of Spanish settlers would enter No Man's Land after each of the failed filibusters. With each defeat of the revolutionary forces, the royalist forces would seek their revenge on the people they saw as traders, killing, raping, pillaging and torturing suspected revolutionaries. Often even those who were not involved were targeted in these raids, and many fled for their lives before the royalist army. The first major wave of refugees took place after the defeat of the Gutiérrez-Magee Expedition at the Battle of Medina in 1813 and the brutal reprisals by the royalist forces. Although these refugees would settle throughout No Man's Land, a number would settle in an area about two miles west of the old site of the Presidio Los Adaes and founded the village of Adaes (sometimes referred to as the Spanish village or Old Spanish Town). The largest number of settlers came from Nacogdoches, with a large number coming from San Antonio, La Bahia and Trinidad de Salcedo. At least some of the refugees were former residents who were born and raised at Los Adaes before the forced exile to San Antonio. Many of the other inhabitants had come to Texas from Mexico and were also forced to flee ahead of the Spanish army. It appears that the former Nacogdoches residents lived mostly in the center of the village, while former San Antonio residents—such as Francisco Arocha, José Francisco Ruiz, Mariano Rodríguez and Vicente Tarin—lived on the outskirts of the village. Other non-Hispanic refugees who survived the battle and reprisals, including Anglo American, Irish and Italian refugees, settled on lands near the village, but the character of the village itself was Hispanic.[62]

Many of these refugees who settled the Spanish village were born at Los Adaes and endured the forced migration to San Antonio. These settlers experienced almost forty years of upheavals and forced migrations, as an 1820 deposition by a former Los Adaes soldier, Pedro Procla (Procella), recounts:

> *The abandonment of the Adizes [sic] was forced: the inhabitants were obliged to leave their crops in the month of June, and were not permitted to gather them; two or three families who were sick remained; the government did not take their lands. The inhabitants went to St. Antonio. Captain y Barbo went to Mexico form there and made a representation to the viceroy, who permitted them to return to Trinity. From there they went to Nacogdoches, and the revolution has driven them here.*[63]

The Reverend Timothy Flint visited the village in 1824 and recorded:

> *We went out of the great road, Camino Real, as it used to be called, to visit the Spanish village of Adayes [sic]. It is a curious collection of great, upright log houses, plastered with mud, and having an appearance very different from a French village of the same character. The church was a mean log building with four bells, some of them cracked….*
>
> *It is a curiosity to see them make their bread. It is made from maize that has been boiled in weak lye, which takes off the outer coat. The women have a couple of stones, the one concave and the other convex. The corn is placed in the cavity; they mash it and grind it to an impalpable paste and work the paste into cakes in their hands, managing the whole process and keeping time to a certain tune. One woman will in this way grind and bake so as to keep six men in bread during their meal.*[64]

Another visitor to the village almost a decade later was the Reverend Benjamin Chase, who visited in 1833 on his way to Texas. At that time, there were about three hundred people living in or near the village. Chase wrote about *the extraordinary Spanish village of Adasoes [sic], about three leagues northwest of Natchitoches. So totally distinct and different from anything else found in the United States. Houses, streets, manners, and customs all Spanish with an air of the 17th century. Apparently as complete as though taken from Spain and transplanted on the spot where it now is, without disturbing anything.*[65]

The last published description of the village was given in May 1836 by an unnamed soldier from the Sixth Regiment, United States Infantry, on their way to Fort Jesup. He wrote:

Between Natchitoches and Fort Jesup, there is a little Spanish town of some 50 inhabitants, and although they appeared to have an abundance around them, they would not sell a chicken to support us on our journey. The houses are built in the Spanish style, of logs, and a small chapel, of the same materials, contains half a dozen broken bells.[66]

After Mexico won its independence from Spain, some of the residents of the village of Adaes and other refugees in No Man's Land began to slowly return to Texas. It appears that those refugees from San Antonio left first, as many had already sold their lands before 1823. Those from other areas, especially Nacogdoches, took longer to return, many doing so as late as 1827, and some did not return to Texas at all. After the Texas Revolution, there was a great deal of racism toward Hispanic residents, and some returned to Louisiana, settling along the Sabine River and the village of Adaes. After the failed Cordova Rebellion of 1838, when Hispanic settlers in Texas rebelled against the Texas government, several of the participants avoided capture by fleeing to Louisiana. After 1850, the village of Adaes was largely abandoned, as the settlers moved either back to Texas or a few miles north to New Spanish Town. By the late 1800s, New Spanish Town was also abandoned as the Anglo settlements of Marthaville and Robeline were founded. The Spanish community shifted a few more miles away to the western shore of Spanish Lake, where they have remained to the present.[67]

During the colonial period, a number of Lipan Apache were brought into the Spanish and French colonial settlements to serve as enslaved laborers. In the early 1700s, the Lipan Apache of Central and South Texas were caught between the Wichita to the north and east and the Comanches to the north and west. Pushed farther south, the Lipan soon came into contact and conflict with the Spanish. Spain, with limited resources on the frontier, adopted a

Unlike English- and American-style homes, Spanish-style homes (like this one, under construction as part of a demonstration at Los Adaes State Historic Site) were built with upright poles instead of horizontal ones. *Photo by author.*

policy of using Native Americans to fight against each other. Originally, the raids against the Lipan were an attempt to deter them from settling in Spanish territory, but soon, the raids were targeted at capturing the Lipan to be sold into slavery. In 1747, the French negotiated a truce between the Comanche and the Wichita, which opened a three-way trade on the frontier: the French traded weapons in exchange for produce from the Wichita and Caddo and horses, mules and captives from the Comanche. Soon there was a sizeable Lipan population in both the French colony at Natchitoches and the Spanish colony of Los Adaes. Over time, there was a great deal of intermarriage between the Europeans and the Native Americans. When Los Adaes was closed in 1773, the entire population was ordered to San Antonio. Unhappy there, Antonio Gil Ybarbo led many of the Adaesanos back to East Texas, founding Nacogdoches in Texas and the community that would become Ebarb in modern Sabine Parish. By 1819, there were culturally Spanish settlements at Bayou Pierre, Bayou Scie (sometimes referred to as Vallecillo; the modern Zwolle area) and in the area of Adaes. There were also Spanish settlers on the Las Ormegas grant and at the Three Prairies (which are located north of Ebarb and still called these names by older residents).[68]

During the 1790s, the Spanish invited several Native tribes, including the Choctaws and Coushatta, to settle in Louisiana to act as a buffer between the Americans who were pushing westward and Spanish Texas. After the Louisiana Purchase, many of these tribes moved into Spanish-controlled Texas (which included western Louisiana). Many of the Choctaw settled in existing Native communities like Ebarb, which had a mixture of Spanish and Lipan Apache who began to intermarry, leading to the creation of the Choctaw Apache Tribe, which received State Recognition in 1978.[69] The Louisiana Coushatta settled along the Red River, but in an effort to avoid American settlers, a group of about 250 migrated to the Calcasieu River in 1861, and in the 1880s, a group of roughly 300 Coushatta settled at Bayou Blue.[70]

The African American experience in the Neutral Strip would not have been a pleasant one, and as a result, there were few African Americans in the region before the Civil War. The creation of the Neutral Strip made it dangerous for African Americans, because while there were laws in the United States that provided some level of protection for both free people of color and enslaved persons, those limited laws did not apply in No Man's Land. Many a free person of color who crossed into No Man's Land was attacked; if they had papers proving their free status, the papers would be destroyed, and the free person of color would be sold back into slavery. Runaways continued to try and cross the Neutral Strip, but now they had to dodge not only the people chasing them, trying to return them to slavery, but also bands of outlaws, who often would treat them less humanely than the patrols sent to find them—at least those patrols needed them alive and healthy to collect their reward, whereas the outlaws had no such restrictions. The saddest state was of those who were smuggled from Texas into Louisiana, as they were often taken off Spanish ships or Spanish colonies and spoke little to no English, had no idea where they were or what was going to happen to them, were already malnourished and then were forced to cross No Man's Land through swamps and forests, as the smugglers had to avoid even the most rudimentary trails to keep their plans to pass the enslaved off as runaways a secret.[71]

Once No Man's Land became part of the United States, some African Americans were brought to the region as enslaved persons. While there were very few large slave owners in the area, there were a number of people who owned a dozen or fewer African Americans. In the post–Civil War era, many formerly enslaved people would stay in the region, making their living as small-scale farmers. A large influx of African Americans would move into

No Man's Land in the late nineteenth and early twentieth centuries, seeking employment with the railroads and lumber mills.

A surprising number of the early settlers of No Man's Land were the former outlaws themselves. Apparently, even outlaws need a retirement plan, and those who were not killed needed a place to settle where questions about one's past were not often asked. There are many stories, family histories and legends of an outlaw turning away from his former life, either because of a narrow escape, "earning" enough gold and goods, falling in love or having a change of heart. No Man's Land was a convenient place for these men to settle, as not only were they familiar with the land and lifestyle, but it was also a region where no one asked too many questions about a man's past.

Even before the United States chased Jean Lafitte off Galveston Island in 1821, many of his associates had already settled in the lower part of No Man's Land along the Sabine and Calcasieu Rivers, with many more settling there after 1821. Some of the former captains still offered services to Lafitte's organization, such as providing trading posts between Lafitte and the residents, supplies and food for Lafitte's crews and convenient hiding places when they were being chased by authorities. Lafitte's organization was an important link for the settlers in No Man's Land, as they provided many manufactured goods that were difficult to acquire but vital for survival in the Neutral Strip in exchange for the food and forest products that Lafitte's crews needed. Some of Lafitte's associates who are known to have settled in No Man's Land were Jean's brother Pierre, who settled on the Sabine, William Smith, Arsene LeBleu, John Ayres, Latney Parrott, Raymond Daley, Henny Griffith, Michel de Rivière (Pithon), Catalon and Wash (who were both former slaves), James Campbell, Jean Baptiste Callistre, Henny Perry, Charles Sallier, Pierre Guilotte, Henri Núñez and Burrill I. Franks. Charles Cronea (who became famous as the last living member of Lafitte's crew) reportedly lived in the area of modern Calcasieu before returning to Galveston Island. Jean Lafitte drops out of history soon after he was chased out of Galveston by the U.S. Navy at the request of the Spanish. Some believe he died in 1825 on a small island in the Gulf, others believe he went north to hide and a few believe he hid in the swamps of Louisiana until his death.[72]

Two of Lafitte's associates would play important roles in the founding of Calcasieu Parish and Lake Charles. Arsene LeBleu, who was born in 1783, inherited 640 acres along the Calcasieu River. He settled on a spot about five to ten miles east of present-day Lake Charles, which soon grew into a village known as LeBleu Settlement, which had a thriving cattle trade between the settlement and Opelousas, as well as being a popular waystation for travelers and traders going to Texas. One of the early settlers of LeBleu Settlement was Charles Sallier, who arrived in Louisiana from France, in 1790. Charles apparently wandered through Louisiana and East Texas until he met and married Arsene LeBleu's sister Catherine in 1802. Charles and his new wife eventually settled on a large lake, which would come to be called Charley's Lake and later became known as Lake Charles. Charles and Lafitte soon became trading partners, with Lafitte depending on Charles's home as an important supply point and hideout. According to local history, on at least one occasion, Lafitte's ship was being pursued by the authorities, so he sailed up to Charles's home, took the cannons and some of the treasure off his boat and sank it in the lake, then quickly built a dirt barricade for the cannons to fight off the authorities. However, the authorities never came, and Lafitte soon returned with another ship and loaded it up with the cannons and treasure. Because of this story, the hill that Charles's home was on soon became known as Money Hill. Of course, there is the matter of the treasure left on the sunken boat and what may have been buried on Money Hill, but so far, if a treasure hunter ever discovered it, they have kept it to themselves.

Unfortunately, tragedy would soon strike, as Charles came to believe that Lafitte was having an affair with his wife. Two stories with the same ending but different details survive. In one, Charles had been traveling for about four months without sending word, and during his absence, Lafitte came to visit. Catherine was five months pregnant at the time and feared that her husband was dead. Lafitte's daughter, who was with him, gave Catherine her necklace with a gold brooch to cheer Catherine up, and Lafitte asked if she wanted to come with him to Galveston until the baby was born or Charles returned. At the same time, Charles walked in and, hearing only that Lafitte wanted Charles's wife to come with him to Galveston, flew into a rage. Charles, bursting into the room without asking what was going on, shot his wife and ran away, never to be seen again. Luckily, the bullet hit her brooch, saving her life. In a similar story, Charles returns later, after Lafitte's visit, and seeing the brooch, assumes it is a gift from Lafitte and a sign of his wife's unfaithfulness. Charles then shoots Catherine and, assuming she is dead, runs away. Again, it is the brooch that saves her life. Catherine would continue to live in the house, raising six children, and soon the area would grow into Charles Town, later becoming the city of Lake Charles.[73]

"Uncle" Bill Smith was another of Lafitte's former crew to settle in No Man's Land after his sailing days were over. He settled in the southern part of the strip and built a large log home for himself during the mid-1800s. Rumor

Joseph Charles Sallier, son of Charles Sallier and Catherine LeBleu Sallier. *Courtesy of McNeese Archives.*

was that he had a large stockpile of gold and other valuables in the house, and one day, two strangers came to visit. They claimed that they were new to the region and wanted to study Uncle Bill's cabin and see how it was built to learn how to build a similar cabin. During the tour, they noticed a crack above his bed, which Bill said would let in a little air after he had closed everything else up for the night. A few nights later, the two strangers went back to the cabin, slipped their rifles through the crack and fired. They heard a scream and, assuming Bill had been killed, ran and hid to bide their time. They attended Bill's funeral and saw a simple wooden coffin lowered into the ground. A few days later, the strangers broke into the cabin to look for the treasure, but they soon heard a scream, and when they turned to look up at the rafters, they saw Uncle Bill, who shouted to them, "No use looking for it, boys. I took it with me." The strangers bolted for the door and were never seen in those parts again.[74]

Despite the region's status as a neutral ground between the United States and Spain, the danger from outlaws and nature and the isolation from "civilized society," No Man's Land attracted many settlers. When the region finally became part of the United States, those living in the land had to prove they had a legitimate claim on the land, either through a Spanish land grant or having purchased the land from a grant holder. Claimants had to file a petition, appear before a committee with witnesses and testify under oath about how they got the land, how long they'd had it and if they had been actively cultivating it. Of the 280 claimants, only 29 were denied. There were undoubtedly more settlers who never sought legal claim to their land, and some of the Spanish settlers and refugees no doubt went to Mexican Texas without applying for a claim to their Neutral Ground lands.[75] We may never know the exact number of people who lived in the Neutral Strip, but these early settlers proved that a hardworking person could make a living in No Man's Land. Soon these first settlers would be joined by new neighbors, and they would have to learn not only how to live together but also how to be Americans. But No Man's Land becoming U.S. territory did not mean that law and order was immediately restored; in fact, a new breed of outlaw was coming, and it would take over a century for No Man's Land to become "civilized."

CHAPTER 5

LAW AND ORDER?

O n February 22, 1821, exactly two years after it was signed, King Ferdinand VII approved the Transcontinental Agreement. But the agreement only lasted for two days, because on February 24, the king signed a proclamation providing for the independence of Mexico and all the provinces, including Texas. The United States quickly recognized Mexico as an independent country and reaffirmed the boundary at the Sabine River. American troops had occupied Camp Riley for almost three years even without the treaty being ratified, but with the death of Long and a need to reduce the freight costs to supply the force on the Sabine, the troops were removed to Natchitoches to await further orders. With the ratification of the treaty by Mexico in 1821, the era of No Man's Land officially came to end. While the Neutral Strip would soon be open to settlement and would see a wave of travelers heading to Texas, it would be decades before "law and order" would be brought to the region. Louisiana governor Jacques Philippe Villeré pressed the War Department for a permanent military post near the Sabine River to protect the western boundary and help civilize the Neutral Strip.

The position of Fort Claiborne had been chosen in large part for political reasons: since the first post commander, Captain Turner, would also be acting as the civil magistrate, it was felt that the fort needed to be close to town. As the fort was built close to Natchitoches, it was hard to maintain discipline; the location provided the soldier "free scope to indulge himself in all the vices of the age, which in every way seduce him from his duty and ruins his health and dissipates his morality." However, due to the site's proximity to town, high transportation costs and the unhealthiness of the site—which was near a lagoon that, three quarters of the year, contained "a host of musketoes [*sic*]"—plans were made to relocate the garrison, but it would not be until 1816 that official orders were received to establish a new post west of Natchitoches, closer to the Red River. Construction began on Fort Selden in 1816, but for various reasons, work on the post started and stopped several times between 1816 and 1819. Fort Claiborne was closed on July 11, 1819, and the buildings were turned over to various landowners.[76]

When the international boundary was set at the Sabine River, this wild land of outlaws was now part of the state of Louisiana, and the state government immediately began asking the federal government for assistance in protecting the new territory and ending the reign of the outlaws. Governor Jacques Philippe Villeré requested both in 1819 and 1820 that the government establish a military post near the Sabine River. The War Department was unwilling to post permanent troops in the Sabine Valley until the treaty was ratified. Once the boundary was set, the Seventh Regiment of United States Infantry was transferred from the Florida/Georgia border to western Louisiana. They spent the winter of 1821 at Fort Selden, and with the coming of spring, Lieutenant Colonel (and future president) Zachary Taylor and General Edmund P. Gaines began scouting the former Neutral Ground for a location for a major military post. It was decided that a fort halfway between the boundary and

Natchitoches would serve the purpose of guarding the boundary and protecting the settlers and travelers. They selected a spot near the San Antonio Trace, on the highest ground between the two rivers. The fort would be named for Thomas Jesup, who was the quartermaster general of the United States Army and a friend of Zachary Taylor.[77]

Fort Jesup was established at Shield's Spring, which was named for the family of squatters that was living on the land. Both General Gaines and Colonel Taylor believed that all the land in the former Neutral Ground was "public" land, meaning it belonged to the United States until the land could be surveyed and the Spanish land grants authenticated. Even though General

Zachary Taylor circa 1845. Courtesy of Office of State Parks, Fort Jesup State Historic Site.

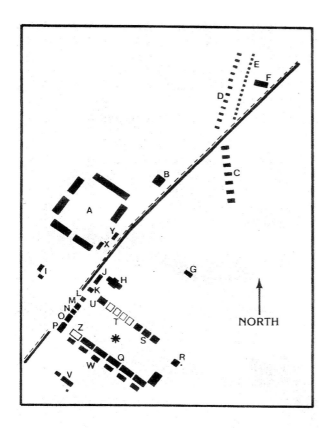

Key

A. Dragoon Stables
B. Stable
C. Blissville
D. Soldiers' Quarters,
   3rd Infantry
E. Officers' Quarters,
   3rd Infantry
F. Mess House 3rd Infantry
G. Officers' Quarters No. 1
H. Officers' Quarters No. 2
I. Officers' Quarters No. 3
J. Store House
K. Powder Magazine
L. Guard House
M. Adjutant's Office,
   3rd Infantry

N. Quarter Master's Office
O. Quarter Master's Store
P. Commissary Store
Q. Soldiers' Quarters
R. Cottage
S. Officers' Quarters (New)
T. Officers' Quarters (Old)
U. Adjutant's Office
V. Hospital
W. Kitchens,
   Soldiers' Quarters
X. Band Quarters
Y. Soldiers' Quarters
Z. Officers' Quarters

*Parade Ground

Map of Fort Jesup.
*Courtesy of the Louisiana
Office of State Parks, Fort
Jesup Historic Collection.*

Reconstructed officers' quarters at Fort Jesup. *Photo by author.*

Gaines was certain that the Shield family had no legal claim to the land, he still ordered they be paid for all the improvements to the land. The Shield family had cleared several acres and erected two or three cabins, which Taylor felt were worth eighty to one hundred dollars.[78]

Taylor ordered Captain George Birch to proceed to Shield's Spring with an advance party of soldiers to begin constructing the post. When a number of the buildings had been finished, Taylor transferred his command from Fort Selden to Cantonment Jesup, arriving on May 13, 1822. The term *cantonment* had a vague meaning even in the early nineteenth century but basically meant a military post built west of the Mississippi, the idea being that these posts were temporary and as settlement moved farther west, the cantonments would move westward with them. Some of the cantonments lasted only a few years, while others, like Jesup, were open for decades. In February 1832, the War Department issued an order clarifying the naming of posts and changed all cantonments to forts, including Fort Jesup. The first garrison was four companies of the Seventh Infantry and numbered 147 officers and men. Within only a few years, Fort Jesup would become the largest military post in Louisiana and, by the 1840s, would be one of the largest west of the Mississippi River, having a garrison of over 1,000 soldiers and more than one hundred buildings.[79]

Fort Jesup enlisted men's kitchen/mess hall. *Photo by author.*

Food was plentiful in the forests, fields and streams of No Man's Land, but diets of the era would have been monotonous, as the types of foods available were seasonal in nature. All foods were cooked over an open fire or in a fireplace. This stone fireplace in the enlisted kitchen at Fort Jesup State Historic Site was built circa 1837. *Photo by author.*

James B. Many. *Courtesy of Town of Many Historical Museum.*

Soldiers from Fort Jesup soon set about their mission of bringing No Man's Land under the control of the United States. As the Spanish settlers' loyalties were uncertain, a detachment of troops was sent to Spanish Lake, remaining there a few months before being recalled when it became obvious that the settlers had no intention of causing trouble. Other soldiers were sent on patrols along the Texas Road and Sabine River, and mapmaking survey parties were sent into the wilderness. Zachary Taylor was soon transferred to the First U.S. Infantry near Baton Rouge, and he was replaced by James B. Many. Many was a native of Delaware who entered the army in 1798 and was a veteran of the War of 1812. In the summer of 1823, he led an expedition to explore and map the Sabine River. Many, along with a captain and twelve privates, built a keelboat (a large, flat-bottomed raft, usually with a deckhouse) that they referred to as "the ark." They sailed down the Sabine River, making maps and charts of depths, navigation obstacles and currents, as well as identifying plants and other resources along the banks of the Sabine. The party encountered bears, wolves, wildcats, panthers, deer and turkeys, and at night "the growling of bears, the howls of wolves, and the screams of the American panther, made the hair of the sturdiest soldiers stand on end."[80] The expedition returned to Fort Jesup in late July, maps in hand, without having lost a single man. Within less than ten years, steamboats would be traveling up and down the Sabine, and the information provided by Many's expedition would prove priceless for opening the Sabine to navigation and settlement. Further improving navigation, over one hundred soldiers from Fort Jesup cleared the Sabine River of logjams and other navigational obstacles in 1837. Fort Jesup soldiers also built and maintained a series of roads that connected Louisiana, Arkansas and Oklahoma. They built a military road roughly 262 miles cut through the forest with hand tools that ran from Fort Jesup to Fort Towson in Oklahoma, and they repaired and maintained the Texas Road, which ran from Natchitoches through Fort Jesup to the Sabine River. While the purpose of these roads was to make moving supplies and troops from fort to fort easier, civilians used the roads to move west, making their journeys easier and opening new areas to settlement.[81]

Fort Jesup's military purpose was to protect the international boundary with Mexico at the Sabine River. However, one of its most important roles would soon become protecting the thousands of settlers who would travel over the old El Camino Real, headed either to Texas or to the former No Man's Land. When Mexico opened Texas to settlement in 1823, it opened the floodgates of migration, as people flocked to the cheap land of Texas. However, for some, the Sabine represented a step too far, as at the last minute they decided to stay in United States territory and settle in the old No Man's Land. Many famous Americans would travel down the Texas Road, through Fort Jesup and on to Texas, such as William Travis, Jim Bowie and Sam Houston, as well as thousands whose names are forgotten by history. Fort Jesup soon became a convenient camping and resupply spot on the road to Texas, as a large military post with hundreds of armed soldiers tended to make even the bravest outlaw think twice about attacking travelers nearby.[82]

Early relations between the Mexicans and the American settlers were cautious but mostly friendly; however, the first major conflict would happen in 1826, when a group of newer settlers became enraged over the election of town officials in Nacogdoches. The disagreement over the election was so intense that the Mexican government got involved and soon invalidated many of the new settlers' land claims. Haden Edwards led the Americans in a revolt, but when other American settlements, such as Stephen F. Austin's colony, did not rise in revolt to join the settlers but instead joined the Mexican force marching toward Nacogdoches, Edwards and his men fled to Louisiana and the safety of the Sabine River, just as the members of early filibusters had done. The 1830 census shows that many of the refuges from the Fredonian Revolt, as the incident became known, would settle in Natchitoches and throughout the former Neutral Strip. Fort Jesup had at least two soldiers who were involved in the revolt. Private Riley deserted to join the revolt for an adventure; however, Private Charles Martin Gray did so to avoid a false charge of disorderly conduct by an officer from another company. Both men fled Nacogdoches before the Mexican army arrived and, after a difficult journey, were able to make their way back to Fort Jesup, where they were both allowed to rejoin their company without punishment.[83]

On November 17, 1831, James Many and the companies of the Seventh Infantry were transferred to Fort Gibson in modern Oklahoma, and Fort Jesup was named the headquarters of the Third United States Infantry under the command of General Henry Leavenworth. Leavenworth was born in Connecticut in 1783. He joined the regular army at the beginning of the War of 1812 after having served in the state militia and soon earned several promotions for bravery and professionalism. He spent much of his career after the war on the frontier, and he was involved in establishing several important frontier forts, including Fort Leavenworth, which was named in his honor. When Leavenworth arrived at Fort Jesup, he was shocked to find out that the boundaries of the fort had never been surveyed or formerly established. Both Gaines and Taylor believed all the land around the fort was government land, so they saw no need to survey the boundary. Leavenworth was angered by the number of squatters, who not only used timber that was needed to keep the over-three-hundred-soldier garrison in firewood but also sold illegal alcohol to his soldiers, which he bemoaned in a letter written on January 13, 1832: "Our men are deserting by Squads—Those whiskey-selling squatters are the cause of it." The final straw was in February 1833, when one of Leavenworth's best soldiers was killed while traveling through the "property" of one of the squatters. Leavenworth requested that four sections of land be purchased for the use of the fort. This was carried out over about a year's time, and soon, the Fort Jesup Military Reservation covered all the land three miles in every direction from the flagstaff, roughly 16,902 acres.[84]

One of the settlers displaced by the expansion of Fort Jesup was Polly Lemon. Little is known about Polly's early life, but at some point, before 1828, she settled northwest of Fort Jesup. In 1828, Congress passed an act allowing the settlers in the former Neutral Ground to claim the land they were living on if they agreed to improve and cultivate it for five years. This act should have given Polly claim to one square mile, about 640 acres, but with the expansion of Fort Jesup, she moved off her land prior to the five-year mark. It appears that Leavenworth promised to ask Congress to either give her $800 for her land or provide her with a tract of land of equal size somewhere else, but his death in 1834 apparently delayed the process, as no one in the military continued the application process to Congress. Unable to write, Polly enlisted the help of a justice of the peace to help her communicate her request for a land patent. The land office for the district at Opelousas denied her claim, based on the fact that it was in the land reserved for Fort Jesup. Next, Polly petitioned Congress for relief for her claim. The issue was brought before Congress in 1836 by Louisiana representative Rice Garland, who wrote, "It was not the intention of the government to take the property of individuals without compensation." However, it would be 1839 before a bill was passed allowing Polly to settle on any unclaimed land in northwest Louisiana, giving her 640 acres. She chose a tract of land in what would become Caddo Parish. Polly Lemon was a rare case in the early nineteenth century, as she was not only a woman who owned land, but she also exercised her legal rights to petition not only the government land offices but Congress as well, despite her lack of formal education.[85]

At least three other landholders were given money or equal tracts of land: William Lescure; Peter Pattison, who acquired his land from a Rio Hondo land claim of Marian Sanchez; and Frederick Williams, who bought the Rio Hondo claim of Hugh McGuffin at a sheriff's sale.[86] An October 1835 report of the buildings on land acquired when Fort Jesup expanded gives an idea of the variety of houses and outbuildings that were built in the former No Man's Land.[87] The report also lists the acreage of each property, which ranged from .83 up to 82 acres.

One dwelling house 40 feet square with out buildings
One good house 73 by 47 with good out buildings
One good house 43 ft square with kitchen adjoining
Three small houses, with stables in shed form
One good stable 60 feet square and good buildings
One house 90 by 36
Four small frame houses, one 34 by 18 and three 48 by 18
Three small frame houses 48 by 18
One dwelling house 2 stories high 52 by 40
One house 96 by 42 and one house 42 feet square
One house 52 by 44 with brick basement and piazza
One house 52 by 44 with brick basement and piazza and wings for a kitchen and outbuildings.
One dwelling house 57 by 44 and one store house 40 feet square
Two small log houses of little value
One store 70 by 40 and one kitchen
One house 100 by 45 with large kitchen in rear [There were 5 properties listed that matched this description, each on .83 acres.]
One house used as an Inn—47 by 39 feet

Located just outside Fort Jesup was an area known as Shawneetown. Saloons, gambling houses, brothels and other entertainments were available for soldiers, travelers and others of questionable morals. It was at Shawneetown that soldiers and settlers could find any illegal or immoral activity. Horse races, boxing, cockfights and "gander pullings" were common. A gander pulling was when an old, tough gander (male goose) was hung by the feet from a pole or branch and heavily greased. After consuming a great

Reproduction of a deck of cards typical of the era from the late 1700s through the early 1800s. Notice that there are no numbers on the cards. *Photo by author.*

deal of alcohol, men would ride their horses as fast as they could toward the goose and try to grab it by the neck. The winner was the one who could grab the neck and pull off the goose's head. However, the alcohol, the heavily greased and flapping goose and the horses' uneven gait ensured that most missed, and many fell off their horses, to the amusement of the crowd of onlookers. As late as 1912, people who passed the site of Shawneetown would recall how many a man spent his last night on Earth there. After Fort Jesup closed, the town lost its largest customer base and was soon abandoned. For most of the nineteenth century, the area was unoccupied. In the 1890s, a small school was built there, but it did not last long, and soon the pine forest reclaimed the site.[88] Once Many High School was built near the site in 1980, the town of Many began to spread to the east, and several subdivisions were built in the area where Shawneetown once stood. Many residents of these subdivisions still report finding artifacts in their yards. There is much debate about where the name came from, and some local residents maintain that it was never called Shawneetown but rather Shantytown.[89]

Even with the attempts to establish law and order in No Man's Land, mob rule was still widespread, often with tragic results. Two former soldiers from Fort Jesup whose last names were Luny and Connel decided to go into the merchandise trade at the end of their enlistments and, using their savings, opened a store. The pair were well liked, and Connel married the daughter of Elisha Robinson, who was one of the most prominent men in the area. At some point, for reasons not recorded, the partnership was dissolved. Luny moved near Ayes Bayou, opened a new store with a different partner and hired a factotum (general employee) who was described as a "half-witted boy." One day, Luny's partner went missing, and the theory that Luny was the only person with a motive soon became widespread throughout the population. The people became more excited the more they talked about the case, and soon, a group of citizens took the boy and began to question him. The boy was terrified by this group, who not so much interviewed him as interrogated him until he agreed that Luny had killed his business partner and thrown the body in the lake. When the lake was dragged, no trace of the body was found, but the citizens had worked themselves up into such a fit that they decided Luny was guilty and should be hanged. Soon, Luny found himself in the hands of the mob. Luny protested his innocence, but since the mob was sure he had committed the crime, they hanged him. Not long after the lynching, the body of his partner was found along a trail in the woods. He was sitting by a tree and had apparently died of a heart attack.[90]

Smuggling continued along the southern part of the old Neutral Ground even after the land became United States territory. The large rivers and bayous along the Gulf Coast made it easy to evade customs officers. In order to stop smugglers from using the Calcasieu River and the associated lakes and streams in the southern part of No Man's Land, the War Department sent a detachment of forty-one soldiers to set up a camp and patrol the lower Neutral Strip. These troops remained in the area from October 1822 to September 1, 1823. By 1829, illicit trade along the Gulf Coast was so rampant that the Treasury Department requested that troops be stationed on the Calcasieu River, and the commanding officer of these troops was to serve as inspector of customs. Colonel James B. Many, in command at Fort Jesup, received orders on November 20, 1829, to send one company of infantry from Fort Jesup to the Calcasieu. Company E, Seventh U.S. Infantry under the command of Captain George Birch, arrived at Lake Charles in January 1830 and remained on station until November 8, 1831, when they were replaced by Company F, Third U.S. Infantry under Captain T.J. Harrison, and stayed there until January 2, 1832, when they were ordered to Fort Jesup.

The camp was referred to as Camp Atkinson in 1822 and as Camp Lake Charles or the Post at Calcasieu until July 1829, when the name was officially set as Cantonment Atkinson. The military post was established on Lake Charles in the northwest part of what would become the town of Lake Charles, on what later became the property of the J.A. Bel Lumber Company. Not long after the camp was abandoned, Thomas Bilbo purchased the property and used the log buildings as his home, expanding them as his family and business grew. The site grew into a center of commerce for what

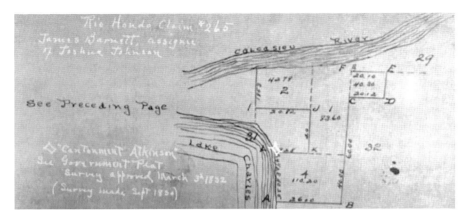

Map of Cantonment Atkinson. *Courtesy of McNeese University Archives.*

would later become the city of Lake Charles, and several of the streets in Lake Charles are named for Bilbo family members. The site is now occupied by the Bilbo family cemetery.[91]

Although the passing of time and the increasing population made travel through No Man's Land a little safer, it was still common to travel in groups. Newcomers to the region were nervous about traveling alone, and not only for fear of outlaws—they also wanted guides to show them the trails and where it was safe to camp. But sometimes, appearances are deceiving, as one traveler, Noah Smithwick, would discover. He had been traveling through Louisiana, but when cholera broke out, he, like many other residents, fled to the pine hills to escape the epidemic. Having a fast horse, he decided to travel to the races held in western Louisiana. As he set out on his journey, he planned to stop at the cabin of a man named Fox "who kept a hostelry for the accommodation of the few chance travelers on that lonely road." The cabin was located between Fort Jesup and Bayou Coti, but it took Smithwick longer than expected to reach the cabin. "Getting late in the day, and seeing no signs of human habitation, I was growing apprehensive of having to make a dry camp, when I saw a little smoke rising some little distance from the road." Riding up, he saw a well-dressed older man, who greeted him "pleasantly." The stranger asked where Noah was going, and when Noah replied that he was going to Fox's, the stranger said he was going there, too, and asked if Noah would like some company for the trip. "Pleased with the appearance of my would-be traveling companion, I readily assented. The next morning, we started on together and I congratulated myself on my good fortune in having fallen into such pleasant company." Later that day, the stranger asked Noah if he would like to know who his traveling companion was, then revealed he was a notorious horse thief who had just gotten out of the penitentiary. Noah was terrified for his life, but not only was the horse thief kind to Noah, he also assured him that he had turned over a new leaf and even took Noah to meet his family. The former horse thief is referred to as Uncle John in Noah's writings, although that was not his real name. Uncle John was apparently quite popular in the community, as everyone they met greeted him warmly. When Noah asked how he had stayed so popular, considering his former line of work, John replied that he never stole from a neighbor, nor would he allow anyone to steal from a neighbor: "He always went out side." Uncle John also taught Noah an important lesson for the trail: if you see a cabin with black smoke coming out of the chimney, that means they are burning too much pine wood, and the food cooked over the fire will not taste good.[92]

With the addition of the Neutral Strip to the United States, settlement increased rapidly. In order to survive in this land, settlers developed close ties with kin and neighbors, who would often share the work of larger jobs, such as house building or daubing (mudding) a chimney. They also banded together for protection and came to each other's aid in times of distress. However, this close-knit family system tended to create a great deal of mistrust of outsiders and sometimes led to violence. While there were some legal land claims, most of the people living in the Neutral Strip were there illegally, and most were squatters. After 1821, most of the settlers coming to western Louisiana were still squatters, setting up a home on any unfenced land. At this time, only small kitchen and herb gardens would be fenced in, to keep animals out of the corn or pea patches near the home. Property lines were not marked with fences, and livestock was allowed to roam free, so it was not necessary to fence in pastureland. Unfortunately for the newcomers, they often ran afoul of those who were already there and who considered the land theirs by right of occupation and the surrounding land their grazing lands. Cattle and hogs were marked so they could be identified when it was time to gather them for butchering, but newcomers were also often unaware of these identification marks and would unwittingly kill someone else's hog or cow, mistaking it for wild, unclaimed livestock. This encroachment on land and livestock often led to violence, as the original settlers would often take the law into their own hands. Most No Man's Landers have at least one story of a family member killed over land or livestock, and often, whole communities would become involved in these feuds. Feuds became even more common over the next several decades as the population increased.[93]

Cattle raising and cattle drives would become an important part of the economy of the former No Man's Land. The Beef Trail (often called the Beef Road) ran from Texas to Alexandria, with branches running throughout East Texas and West Louisiana. These paths were used by cattle drivers to move goods and cattle, horses and swine from the woods and prairies of Texas to larger markets in Louisiana, such as Natchitoches, Opelousas or Alexandria, where they would be purchased and taken to New Orleans for shipment around the world. Austin's colony was a major supplier of the beef that traveled down this route. Often, there would be "stands" along the path, where cattle could be pastured to rest, get fresh water and regain some of the weight they lost on the trail. The drivers would also be able to resupply, as there were trading posts nearby to sell needed items to the cattlemen. The stands were spaced about ten miles apart (about a day's ride on the trail) and were often near waterways, as "swimming the herd" was the most difficult and dangerous part of the journey. Experienced cowhands had tricks to make these crossings easier, such as not crossing when the cows would be facing the sun, as the animals would get spooked if they saw their reflections in the water. Over time, ferries would be established along these routes, which would charge a fee

Burr's Ferry. *Courtesy of Vernon Parish History.*

Pendleton Gaines Ferry. *Courtesy of Vernon Parish History.*

for carrying the animals across. While the ferries made the crossing easier, they were expensive and time-consuming, since it often took several trips to get an entire herd across.[94]

Settlers with cattle-related skills often settled near the stands, and soon, villages were established. Old Campground, between the Sabine River and Alexandria, was one such stand, and artifacts recovered there show that it was used by early Native Americans, French, Spanish and, later, Americans as a rest stop. Old Campground has one of the oldest, if not the oldest, documented cemeteries in southwestern Louisiana. The site was also popular with Methodist circuit riders, who used the large open areas for revivals and camp meetings. Sugartown was another of these villages that grew from a stand, as Sugar Creek was easy to ford at the point where the village was founded. Sugartown was located a few miles west of Old Campground and was founded around 1816, making it one of the first American villages in southwest Louisiana. Not only was the cattle industry important to Sugartown, but the residents also pooled their resources to construct mills for making flour and sugar and gins for processing cotton. One of the early settlers near the two settlements was "Saddler" Johnson, who earned his name because of his leatherworking skills and was known for his whips, boots and saddles. Although the cattle drives are a distant memory, raising cattle is still an important part of life throughout all of twenty-first-century No Man's Land. Cattle are raised in every parish of the old Neutral Strip, leatherworking is still a popular handcraft, beef is an important food source and many of the foodways of the region are still tied to the beef trails through briskets, chilis and cowboy stews.[95]

With cattle drives came cattle rustling, which would plague No Man's land for decades. During the Neutral Ground era, settlers in the Sabine Strip petitioned both the Spanish and the Americans to send troops to chase out the rustlers. After the strip became American territory, cattle were a primary target for bandits, because they could be stolen in Louisiana and driven across the Sabine, where they were easy to hide in the vast lands of east Texas. During the Civil War, jayhawkers would ride into a farm and drive off the livestock, either to sell or for their own consumption. Often, communities would form groups of "Regulators" to stop the rustlers, but these groups were often as bad as the bandits they were trying to stop. Even as late as 1884, rustling was still such a problem that a group of citizens in Cameron Parish formed a band of Regulators to try and stop the rustlers.[96]

Even with the increased troop numbers in what had been No Man's Land, the area was still a playground for outlaws. In fact, many of the most famous outlaws operated in the region after the official end of No Man's Land. One of the most famous of these outlaws was the "Reverend Devil" John Murrell. Murrell is by far the most talked about and argued about of the No Man's Land outlaws. Sorting fact from fiction is almost impossible because there are as many versions of the story as there are storytellers. There was a John Murrell whose life and criminal activity were covered in newspapers in Tennessee. This Murrell was assumed to be the same John Murrell who was in Louisiana and Mississippi. Some maintain that he was never even in No Man's Land, but there are too many folk stories and oral histories to completely discount his presence in the region. Some maintain that there was a John Murrell but he was not the Tennessee Murrell and lived decades after the Tennessee Murrell died. Many locals will never accept anything less than that Murrell was the king of No Man's Land outlaws. Probably, like all folktales, there is some truth in this story, even if not all the details are true.

According to the stories of Tennessee John Murrell, he was born around 1806 in Williams County, Tennessee. His father was a Methodist circuit rider who was often away for extended periods as he traveled to spread God's word, and his mother ran a boardinghouse. According to the stories, John's mother did not have the same devotion to God that her husband did, and in his absence, the boardinghouse became a brothel. When the children were old enough, their mother taught them to steal from her customers. Both parents wanted their children to learn their morals, and Murrell soon learned the Bible well enough to quote the Old and New Testaments chapter and verse. As one report claimed, Murrell could quote the Ten Commandments while breaking as many of them as possible at one time. He was arrested as a teenager for stealing horses, found guilty and sentenced to being flogged, having his hand branded with "HT" for "horse thief" and spending time in prison (reports range from one to six years). There is dispute over exactly when Murrell was arrested, but it was sometime in the 1820s. At this point, details become harder to confirm. Around the 1820s and 1830s, reports of a John Murrell started appearing along the Natchez Trace in Mississippi and in the old No Man's Land in Louisiana. Some say there is too much distance between the two places for Murrell to have been at both. However, it should be remembered that the Natchez Trace was connected to No Man's Land by an extension of the old El Camino Real and by the Alexandria Road, which were commonly traveled back and forth, so the distance alone should not dismiss the Murrell legend.[97]

The legends of the Murrell of No Man's Land place his activities in a region between the Texas Road and the Kisatchie Hills of what would later become Sabine and Vernon Parishes. He arrived in the area around the 1820s, so he missed the actual Neutral Strip era of no government control; however, the region was still full of criminal activity, with only the garrison of Fort Jesup and a few lawmen to bring order. Murrell posed as a circuit rider and was apparently a real fire-and-brimstone preacher with strong public speaking skills, which were useful in keeping his audience enthralled while his men searched their saddlebags and looted their farms. He preferred to steal using stealth and deceit but was not afraid to kill a man to eliminate a witness to his crimes. One of his favorite sermon props was a set of scales, which he would place in front of him; he would then place a Bible on the scales, telling the congregation that the Bible was the book of judgement and until they gave enough gold and silver coins to tip the scales, they would not be forgiven for their sins, which he would start listing. Then he began telling everyone all the good things he would do with money for "God's Work," even going so far as to have some henchmen in the crowd start the donations and urge others to give even more. Needless to say, no widows, orphans or anyone else in need ever saw the benefits of those offerings. Fine horses, fine saddles, fine livestock and anything else Murrell and his gang could lay their hands on were stolen, and many a man lost his life over a horse or a saddle.

Murrell was also reported to be a notorious slave smuggler who would entice a slave to escape his master with Murrell's help. As part of the plan, Murrell would sell the slave two or three times, then Murrell would promise to help the slave escape up North and give him half the money earned from the scheme. Murrell never followed through on his promise, knowing that the angry masters would soon be on their trail. Instead, it was said that

Murrell would kill the slave, cut open his stomach and fill it with rocks—so the body would sink—then dump it in a deep well or a swamp, to be eaten by alligators. According to the stories, wells were Murrell's favorite hiding places for the bodies of his victims, as they were deep and dark and even if the body floated to the surface of the water, it still could not be seen unless someone looked over the edge of the well. Murrell was rumored to have dozens of wells in hard-to-reach places he used just for hiding bodies.[98]

Another aspect of the Murrell legend that is debated is the size of his gang. Some accounts have the number of his followers as high as 1,200, in several states, including Tennessee, Arkansas, Louisiana and Mississippi, with some reports saying he had gang members as far north as Maryland. According to the legends, these men were organized as a secret society called the Mystic Clan, which combined many of the symbols and rituals of the Masons but was organized for crime. Loyalty to the clan was prized above all, and the rituals were designed to reinforce members' loyalty to the clan and to Murrell. Many times, clan members who had broken an oath by either telling a secret or stealing from the clan would be murdered in front of other clan members as part of a ceremony to keep the rest in line. Clan members used secret signs and symbols to identify safe houses and each other. Some clan members had a special golden medallion that they wore to identify themselves. Homes of clan members and safe houses were identified by a black locust tree bordered by two Spanish dagger plants (yucca plants) in the front yard. In order to hide all the loot that Murrell and his men stole, Murrell set up a series of "banks": caves or other hiding places where the goods and gold could be stored until needed. Murrell was rumored to have one bank a few miles from the site of Los Adaes, another near Midway Station a couple of miles from Fort Jesup and a small one near the community of Clearwater in what would later become Sabine Parish's Ward 2. The largest and most elaborate cave was in the Kisatchie Forrest in what would become Vernon Parish. It was a large, complex cave network in the rocky hills and canyons of Kisatchie near Sheard Branch. The caves were reported to have rooms of various sizes that were used as living quarters and storerooms for supplies and stolen goods; some were large enough to stable horses and mules. The path to these caves was through a thick forest, so a series of secret signs was carved onto rocks and trees to guide gang members to the hideout. Even as late as the 1930s, there were still signs of horse tack, trace chains and leather harnesses in the caves. So many people believed that these were Murrell's caves that in 1942, the U.S. Forest Service decided to dynamite the caves to keep people from getting injured or killed as they looked for buried treasure. The caves at Clearwater also had similar markings, but they were destroyed not by the government but by the treasure hunters themselves. At some point, an overzealous treasure hunter used a water well drilling bit to dig through the roofs of the caves, destroying much of the caves' structure. Some of the entrances of the caves are still visible, and a few of the openings are large enough for a horse and wagon to ride into.[99]

What happened to John Murrell is also debated. The Tennessee Murrell was arrested in 1834 for stealing slaves. A booklet that was published at the time and helped lead to his arrest claimed that John Murrell had planned a multistate slave revolt to create chaos on Christmas Day 1834; while the slaves were revolting and members of the upper class were running for their lives, Murrell and his gangs would sweep into the cities to steal and pillage while law enforcement was distracted. After his arrest, he spent ten years in jail. Murrell died from tuberculosis soon after his release. Local legends, however, offer many other possibilities. Many believe that Murrell hid in Mississippi or Arkansas, where he lived out his life but either was unable to return for his money or had already taken it with him. Some say he took his ill-gotten gains and went to South America or even London to live out his life as a wealthy man, while others say he was killed by members of his own gang, at the hands of either Dan Kimbrell, at McNutt Hill in Rapides Parish, or other gang members near his hideout in Kisatchie.[100]

To dismiss all the claims and legends about John Murrell, as some historians have done, is unwise, because to do so is to ignore the effects the Murrell stories have had on the cultural development of No Man's Land. There are enough stories and oral histories to make a case for a real Murrell who operated in the No Man's Land region; whether it was the same John Murrell from Tennessee or another Murrell is hard to determine, due to the mixing of stories over time. At the same time, it is also unwise to assume that every story is true. By nature, storytelling is an art that includes embellishment and entertainment to captivate an audience. The most entertaining stories are the ones that are repeated the most, regardless of their accuracy. There is also an element involved in storytelling whereby the storyteller displays their "special knowledge" of an event by claiming family connections or knowledge of details that other community members do not have access to, increasing the storyteller's status; however, this special knowledge is not always true or may, at the very least, be an exaggeration. While such embellishment makes it difficult for historians to separate fact from fiction and may make some stories less than historically accurate, the stories' role and importance in the cultural development of a community cannot and should not be overlooked. To this day, stories of outlaws are told throughout the No Man's Land region and play a key role in the identity of No Man's Landers. Almost every family that has been in the region since the nineteenth century has a family story of either an outlaw in the family or a family member who escaped an outlaw through strength or cleverness, was killed by an outlaw or overcame a frontier hardship. These stories, whether historically accurate or not, have come to define the identity of No Man's Landers and exemplify their ability to overcome danger and hardships.

The western side of the Sabine River had its share of outlaws, too, and they often crossed into No Man's Land to avoid lawmen and other outlaws when things got too hot in Texas. Even with the end of the Texas revolution, things did not settle down much on the frontiers, as the Texas government had too much land and too few resources to operate police forces in remote areas. During the 1840s in East Texas, people often had to take the law into their own hands. To protect themselves and to try to stop the lawlessness, the citizens formed a group known as the Regulators. At first, most people were happy with the job the Regulators were doing to stop outlaws, but as the Regulators had no set of laws or standards of evidence and did not answer to any court or form of government, they soon got out of control. Anyone even suspected of a crime could find themselves arrested and executed by the Regulators. Often, the Regulators would turn to torture to get information out of someone, about either a crime they might have committed or other suspected outlaws. As their power grew, so did their reign of terror. In order to stop them, other community members formed a group called the Moderators. While there were good people on both sides who only wanted to bring order and safety to their communities, there were many, both men and women, on both sides who abused their power or even became worse than the outlaws they were supposed to be stopping. Over a period between 1839 and 1844, an untold number of people were killed during what would come to be called the Regulator-Moderator War. Order was mostly restored in 1844 when president of Texas Sam Houston sent in militia troops to force a settlement. During the Mexican War in 1846, many former Regulators and Moderators served in the same volunteer unit raised in East Texas, and this helped ease the tension between the factions. However, not everyone was willing to forgive what had happened during the Regulator-Moderator War, and revenge killings and reprisals would continue for decades. Even though the war was centered on East Texas, it spilled into Louisiana, bringing even more violence to the old No Man's Land. Many in the Sabine Strip crossed into

Texas to join one side or the other, members of Regulator and Moderator gangs hid in No Man's Land and neither side had a problem crossing the river to chase someone or take revenge on the family members of an opposing gang member.[101]

Even after almost two decades, Fort Jesup was still assisting in the capture of outlaws. In the summer of 1842, several citizens requested the assistance of members of the Second United States Dragoons (mounted cavalry troops) from Fort Jesup in the capture of Pharoah Hiram Midkiff and James "Tiger Jim" Strickland. Strickland had grown up in No Man's Land and apparently been involved in many crimes and atrocities in Shelby and Harrison Counties in Texas during the Regulator-Moderator War. He barely escaped with his life after being wounded in a shootout and returned to Louisiana to recover and hide. Hiram Midkiff was rumored to have been in the Mystic Clan, but many of his descendants refute this claim. Midkiff was born in Tennessee sometime between 1801 and 1804. In 1818, his family left Tennessee for the Louisiana-Texas borderlands. Midkiff was in San Augustine at least by 1824 and may have been involved in the Moderator–Regulator War in Texas before crossing the Sabine and settling near what would become the village of Fisher in modern Sabine Parish. At this point in the story, the details become contested. The traditional story is that Midkiff was a notorious horse thief who stole and sold horses on both sides of the Sabine River. One day, he set his sights on the horse of Henry Stoker. Midkiff planned to have one of Stoker's slaves steal the horse for him and bring it to a location where Midkiff would be waiting. Apparently, the slave informed Stoker of the plan, because Stoker set a trap for Midkiff: the slave delivered the horse as promised, but then Stoker and his sons shot Midkiff. Some historians say that Midkiff was shot in the act of stealing the horse himself. The *Daily Picayune* reported on July 29, 1842, that Midkiff (spelled "Metcalf" in the article) and Strickland were ambushed by "a party consisting of some citizens and a few dragoons from Fort Jesup" at their hideout on Toro Creek. According to the article, the party encircled the cabin during the night, and when Strickland walked out in the morning, they ordered him to surrender. When Strickland tried to flee, he was shot and killed. Midkiff was wounded in the exchange. When the soldiers and citizens entered the cabin, "the house was full of arms," and a slave who had been stolen in August 1841 was also found. Most of the stories agree that Midkiff was wounded in a gunfight and taken back to Fort Jesup, where he died a few days later from his wound. Midkiff family history holds that Hiram Midkiff was buried at Fort Jesup.[102]

Left: Reproduction dragoon uniform, on display at Fort Jesup SHS. *Photo by author.*

Below: Reproduction dragoon saber, on display at Fort Jesup SHS. *Photo by author.*

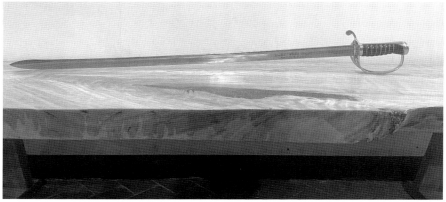

Another band of No Man's Land outlaws with Murrell connections was the Yocum gang, led by Doc Yocum. Supposedly, Doc Yocum acquired a large tract of land from a Revolutionary War veteran whom he cared for and gave room and board—but as soon as the veteran signed over the land, Yocum killed him. Ending up in No Man's Land, Doc Yocum and his family soon began robbing and rampaging along the Sabine River. The gang centered its operations near the Niblett's Bluff area, often lying in wait to rob the cattle traders who were returning with pockets full of cash from the sale of their cattle. Doc Yocum—who, according to legend, was often being pursued by the authorities—used the ferry at Niblett's Bluff to cross into Texas to hide out anytime the pursuers got too close. The Yocums were rumored to have opened a boardinghouse called Yocum's Inn near the ferry and often robbed their guests. Legends are unclear about whether the Yocums were part of the Mystic Clan or simply friendly with the Murrell gang. Several members of the Murrell gang were supposedly members of the Yocum gang, but it is not clear if these members joined after the end of the Mystic Clan, if they were working for both the Yocums and Murrell or if the Yocums worked for Murrell.[103]

Although the area that was to become DeSoto Parish would be settled later then other parts of No Man's Land, it, too, would have outlaw activity. With no major trails running through the parish, there was not as much to attract settlers. Once steamboats began traveling up and down the Sabine River, the area around Shreveport began to grow, and so did the area of DeSoto Parish. One area that was considered especially dangerous because of outlaw activity was the community of Waterloo, which would later be called Logansport. Stories survive of outlaws and smugglers using the area as a base of operations, and woe to the law-abiding citizen who stumbled onto their operations by accident.[104]

In 1844, Fort Jesup would begin its most important role as the headquarters for Major General Zachary Taylor's Army of Observation. After almost a decade of debate in both the United States Congress and the Republic of Texas Congress over whether Texas should join the United States, the Republic of Texas voted to join the Union. During the negotiations, Mexico threatened to declare war on the United States and reconquer Texas. To protect Texas during the process, one third of the United States Army was sent to western Louisiana and stationed at Fort Jesup and Camp Salubrity near Natchitoches. For the next year, over one thousand soldiers were stationed at Fort Jesup, and Taylor used this time to begin training the army under his command. In June and July 1845, troops began leaving Fort Jesup to guard the new boundary between Texas and Mexico. The treaty ending the Texas revolution stated that the Rio Grande was the boundary between Texas and Mexico, but Mexico claimed that the Nueces River was the boundary. American troops landed at Corpus Christi north of the Nueces, but in the spring of 1846, Taylor's forces were ordered to cross the Nueces and occupy the northern bank of the Rio Grande. Mexican forces crossed the river and ambushed a detachment of Second Dragoons, starting the Mexican War. After a year and a half, the U.S. Army captured Mexico City and negotiated a peace treaty whereby the southern boundary of Texas was set at the Rio Grande River and the southwestern states of California, New Mexico, Colorado, Utah and Arizona were added to the United States.

With the annexation of Texas, the frontier moved from the Sabine River to the Rio Grande, and Fort Jesup was no longer needed as a frontier fort. The last troops left Fort Jesup in February 1846. Eventually, the buildings and land would be sold, and a large farming community would develop where the old post had been. The history of Fort Jesup was so important to not only Louisiana but also American history that the site has been named a National Historic Landmark by the United States Congress, the highest honor Congress can give to a property, and the site is preserved as a State Historic Site managed by the Louisiana Office of State Parks. For almost a quarter century, the men of Fort Jesup protected settlers and travelers moving through No Man's Land, mapped and explored the region, built roads that aided travelers moving west, helped opened the Sabine and Red Rivers for navigation and brought the region of No Man's Land under the physical control of the United States. As a military post, Fort Jesup was a training ground for many of the officers who would become generals during the Civil War. The post was either home to or visited by dozens of famous Americans, including Zachary Taylor, Ulysses S. Grant, James Longstreet, William J. Hardee, Henry Leavenworth, David E. Twiggs, Jim Bowie, William Travis, Dred Scott (who would become a famous early civil rights leader) and many more. Over forty officers from Fort Jesup would end the Civil War with the rank of general. Fort Jesup helped bring law and order to the Neutral Ground and guarded the international boundary for almost twenty-five years, then played a key role in the expansion of the territory of the United States to the Pacific Ocean.[105]

With the annexation of Texas and the "settling down" of the Louisiana/Texas boundary, the number of settlers moving into the old Neutral Strip increased. Trouble was bound to break out between the older settlers and these new settlers. One of the best examples of this violence was what became known as the Rawhide Fight. In the 1850s, new settlers began moving into the Walnut Hill region, near modern-day Leesville. Apparently, the community had come together enough to build a schoolhouse, but when the school burned before it even opened, tempers ran high. Some believed that the school was burned by a student who did not want to go to school, and the community divided into factions based on if they thought he was guilty or innocent. One legend claims that a young man was planning to get married, but when his father learned there would be a school in their community, he told his son that the wedding would be postponed until the young man finished school, so he burned down the school in order to get married. Others believed that some in the community did not want their children to go to school because they needed them on the farm, and still others say that the argument was over which group was going to control the school and/or who was going to be able to attend.

Whatever the reason for the fire, it split the community. In order to calm things down, a meeting was called at a local trading post owned by a Mr. Burton and a Mr. Hawkins, but rather than bring the community together, the meeting would end in violence. At some point during the meeting, a fight broke out, and before long, six were dead and an unknown number were wounded. The incident went down in history as the Rawhide Fight because the dead bodies were laid out on large cowhides, called rawhides, that were for sale at the store. Five of the six men killed were Charles Weeks, Mr. Harrison, Mr. Hawkins (who owned the store), Mr. Hardcastle and Mr. Simon. The sixth name has been lost over time. One of the wounded men who escaped was L.C. Sweet. He was taken to another town to hide and recover and was lodging in the home of one Mr. LaCaze. A search party soon arrived at the home and asked LaCaze if they could search the building. LaCaze agreed but asked that they not go into one room, which contained the belongings of his deceased wife. They agreed to the request and, not finding Sweet, rode on to another house. Of course, Sweet was hiding in the room LaCaze asked the men not to search. When Sweet recovered from his wounds, he moved on and eventually settled in Jasper, Texas, where he is buried.[106]

The identity of many of the victims of outlaws in No Man's Land will never be known. Most were travelers passing through on a journey that could take months. Most often, no one was waiting on them where they were going, meaning it could be months before any relatives or neighbors even realized the victims were missing. By then, there was little trace of the victims; the bodies were disposed of (often in a well or deep marsh), any valuables were sold and there were rarely any witnesses outside of the gang. However, one victim who is known was Eli Kay. Eli and his brother Wiley arrived in the area that would become Vernon Parish sometime between 1843 and 1846. According to rumor, they had to leave the Edgefield District of South Carolina after involving themselves in a vigilante mob that killed fourteen slaves. Wiley later moved on and became sheriff of Shelby County, Texas, but Eli settled near Anacoco Creek and became a cotton farmer. On December 11, 1850, while returning from a cotton-selling trip to Natchitoches, Eli was ambushed near Hornbeck and killed, along with his small child in the wagon. It is not known if someone knew he was going to sell his crop and lay in wait to ambush him because of the large amount of money he would have on him or if Eli was just a random target of opportunity, but either way, robbery was the motive for his murder.[107]

Life would settle down some in No Man's land in the 1850s as more settlers came to the area, more roads were built and steamboats moved up and down the Sabine River. There were still many dangers, both from nature and criminals, but twenty years of "civilizing" influences from churches, communities and local governments was beginning to tame the region. But in 1861, the relative peace of No Man's Land would be broken by the Civil War. Soon, old scores and grudges would flare up again, and just like the nation, No Man's Land would be torn apart by pro-Northern and pro-Southern feelings. Violence would break out across the region, and criminal activity would skyrocket as officials were distracted by the Civil War. It would be well into the twentieth century before a level of law and order would be returned to No Man's Land.

CHAPTER 6

DAILY LIFE IN NO MAN'S LAND

The first American settlers came to No Man's Land in search of free land. Most of the settlers were poor farmers from other southern states who could not afford the rising land costs in the more settled areas. Bringing their families and a few tools, they cleared the land, planted crops and built their own homes. The settlers braved many hardships; shortages, including a lack of manufactured goods and medical care; all the dangers of nature, like storms, floods and dry spells; and wild animals such as bears, wolves, snakes and alligators, plus the bands of outlaws that roamed the land.

When settlers arrived, their first task was building a shelter for themselves and their families. The forests provided almost all the resources they needed for building their first homes. Depending on the amount of time they had and the skills of the homebuilder, cabins could be rudimentary or elaborate. If a cabin had to be thrown up quickly, a simple one-room structure with rounded logs would be built. However, rounded logs rotted faster in the humid climate of Louisiana and had larger gaps that would have to be filled with mud mixed with straw or Spanish moss, which took up more time and had to be replaced often. As time and resources allowed or as families grew, more rooms would be added or new cabins would be built, with the earlier cabins usually being turned into barns or storehouses or torn down so the materials could be reused. The most common design was the dog trot, which would have an open hallway with rooms on either side and a large porch at the front and back. The open hall would allow breezes to help cool the cabin, and the porches and hall provided shaded areas for doing work during

Early nineteenth-century draw knife. *Courtesy of the Louisiana Office Fort Jesup Historical Collection. Photo by author.*

the heat of the day and for sleeping on hot, humid nights. Some chimneys were made of bricks, but many were made of sticks stacked together and covered in clay. The clay was allowed to harden, and the heat from the fires continued to harden the clay. However, old-timers often warned children and newcomers not to let the fire get too high in the chimney, as it could light the smaller, more flammable sticks near the top of the chimney on fire. Many of these log cabins were still being used as homes in the 1970s, and many were still standing in the 1990s. Unfortunately, time and neglect has caused most to be lost to time.[108]

Settlers started building their cabins by cutting logs with a felling axe. Once the tree was down, a barking iron, which was a long pole with a sharp, flat blade at the end, would be used to remove the bark from the log. In humid climates, the bark allowed moisture to stay in the wood, causing rot, and it allowed bugs to bore into the wood, speeding up the rotting process. Next, a broadaxe would be used to square the log. The broadaxe was different from a regular axe in that it was flat on one side, allowing the cutter to get the blade very close to the log. Once the log was squared, a foot adze would be used to smooth out the log and remove any rough bumps that were left. The adze had a carved blade and was called a foot adze because the cutter would swing the blade close to his foot and lift the front of his boot, so that if he missed the log, it would hit the sole of his shoe (which had the thickest leather) instead of his leg. Next, notches would be cut in the ends of the logs to allow a tight fit to hold the logs together once they were stacked on top of each other. To make shingles for the roof, the settler would usually cut down a cedar or cypress tree and cut it into blocks. These blocks would then be cut using a froe, a long metal blade that had a wooden handle forming a ninety-degree angle. A maul (basically a wooden club) would be used to hammer the froe into the block of wood, splitting off a thin, flat board. That board would then be taken to a shaving horse, which was a

Dog Trot house at Pleasant Hill, Louisiana. This cabin was built sometime before the Civil War. *Photo by author.*

Log cabin at Florien, Louisiana. Built circa 1859. *Photo by author.*

This page, top: Early nineteenth-century broadaxe. *Courtesy of the Louisiana Office of State Parks, Fort Jesup Historical Collection. Photo by author.*

This page, bottom: Early nineteenth-century adze. *Courtesy of the Louisiana Office Fort Jesup Historical Collection. Photo by author.*

Opposite, top: Volunteers at Fort Jesup SHS demonstrating how the shaving horse works. *Photo by author.*

Opposite, bottom: Close-up view of notches on the log cabin at Florian. *Photo by author.*

bench that had a block of wood that held the shingle in place. A draw knife (a curved blade with handles on both sides) was used to smooth the shingle down so that it would fit tightly, forming a waterproof seal. It would take several dozen trees to make the walls for the cabin—hundreds of shingles— plus several more trees to make doors, shutters, rafters and pegs. Window glass was rare, so windows were either open holes that could be closed by

shutters or would have a screen made of an animal hide that had been scraped thin enough that it allowed light to pass thorough but kept out some of the bugs.[109]

At the beginning of the nineteenth century, handmade items were more common than manufactured ones. With the beginning of the industrial revolution in the United States in the 1820s, the number of factory-made items steadily increased. However, in No Man's Land and along the frontier, high transportation costs limited their availability, so settlers had to learn to use natural resources to make many of the items they needed, including bowls, plates, cups, toys and cooking utensils. These items were often made of wood, animal horn or plants like gourds. Even as late as the mid-twentieth century, it was common to have residents of a community who carved wooden bowls or made and used gourd spoons and dippers. Unfortunately, many of the traditional crafts are being lost with the passage of time.

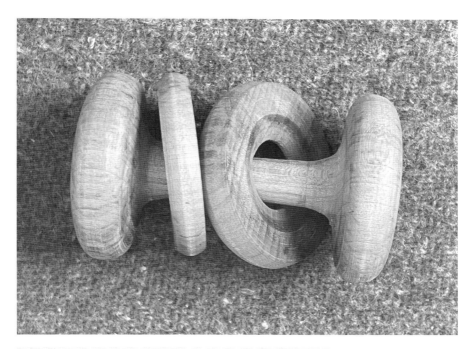

Opposite: Early nineteenth-century froe (*left*) and a hand-carved reproduction maul. *Courtesy of the Louisiana Office Fort Jesup Historical Collection. Photo by author.*

Above: Handmade wooden baby rattle. *Photo by author.*

Left: Canteen made from a gourd. *Photo by author.*

Top: Handmade wooden spoon. *Bottom*: Spoon made from a cow's horn. *Photo by author.*

Before the 1830s, the most common manner of eating food in the United States was to use a two-tine fork to hold the food in place to cut it and use the point of a knife to bring the food to the mouth. This practice, referred to as the "American" fashion by Europeans, was common for both men and women of all ages, even small children, and across all social classes. Starting in the 1830s and gaining popularity in the 1840s and 1850s, many members of higher society began adopting the "European" fashion of using the fork to bring the food to the mouth. Soon forks with three or four tines would become common. This method continued to gain popularity throughout the 1800s, until it become commonplace by the twentieth century.[110]

As new frontiers were opened, tableware generally progressed from wooden trenchers and plates to dishes made of pewter, then to locally produced ceramics (often referred to as earthenware) then the more refined imported ceramics. While the cost of transportation tended to make imported ceramics less common on the frontier, most homes that wished to be seen as fashionable had at least some imported ceramics. The most popular form of ceramic between the late eighteenth through the mid-nineteenth century was known as creamware and was basically plain white. Pearlware, which was white with a bluish tint, was one of the most common in the early 1800s. It was nearly always decorated with a colored

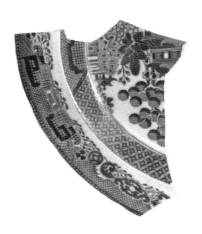

Top, left: Fragment of blue transferware recovered near one of the officer's homes at Fort Jesup. *Photo by author.*

Top, right: Fragment of a blue-edged pearlware plate recovered near one of the officer's homes at Fort Jesup. *Photo by author.*

Bottom: Brown transferware cup recovered near one of the officer's homes at Fort Jesup. *Photo by author.*

edge and often referred to as shell-edged or edged ware. After the War of 1812, transferware become popular and often depicted scenes from exotic lands, romantic landscapes or ancient ruins. In the 1820s, dark blue was the most popular color. In the 1830s and 1840s, additional colors such as red, green and brown also became popular. By the 1850s, transferware had declined in popularity.[111]

Homes of this era, even those of upper-class families, were not well lit. Candlesticks were expensive, and candles were time-consuming to make. The cheapest and most common candles were those made of tallow, processed animal fat that was made during butchering and used for cooking, candlemaking and soapmaking—and that, when burned as candles, produced an unpleasant smell. Beeswax candles had a better smell when burned, but on the frontier, beeswax was harder to acquire. Often, frontier housewives would mix beeswax and tallow to make the beeswax go further and weaken the strong smell of the tallow. Paraffin wax was developed in Germany in 1830 but would not be available on the frontier for more several years. Until 1825, candlewicks were made of loosely spun strands of cotton. These wicks were cheap, but they made the candle harder to relight due to carbon buildup and were not totally consumed. Therefore, it was important to use a candlesnuffer to extinguish the flame, and the wick had to be trimmed during use and after it was extinguished so that it could be used again. The tightly braided wick that was treated with a mineral material (which is still used today) was developed in France in 1825, and it revolutionized candle production, as now the wick was self-consuming and no longer had to be constantly trimmed. These wicks were soon available throughout the United States. Along the East Coast, lamps that burned whale oil were becoming common, but whale oil was difficult to acquire on the frontier, so until the 1850s, oil lamps were rare. Kerosene oil was developed in 1846 as a cheaper substitute for whale oil and was distilled from coal (some old-timers still call it coal oil). Lamps that burned either kerosene or paraffin would become commonplace after the Civil War throughout the United States, even in No Man's Land.[112]

Women's everyday clothing in the early nineteenth century consisted of a series of layers. A lady's main undergarment was a chemise, also known as a shift. It was a long gown that was worn both night and day. It was never worn in public without a bodice or a gown covering it. The next layers would be several skirts and a bodice. An apron would always be worn during the day while working to protect the clothes, as most women only had two or three sets of clothes. During colder weather, women would wear more layers

Volunteers at Fort Jesup SHS portraying women's life on the trail. They are wearing chemises, skirts and bodices. *Photo by author.*

of chemises and skirts to stay warm. Because these garments were made of whatever materials were available, the colors often did not match the way we think of today.

Starting in the 1790s, clothing for more formal events and social calls began to be of the empire style, based on the latest fashions in France. These dresses had tighter-fitting skirts, higher waistlines and lower necklines. For ladies of high society, dresses were usually white with colored accents and made of delicate cloth. On the frontier, these fashions were often copied, but the materials were either homespun or more durable materials. With the beginning of the industrial revolution, factory-made materials with colored prints became more available. The fashion remained popular until the late 1820s, being replaced by dresses with lower waistlines and fuller skirts in the 1830s.[113]

Men's fashions of the era, even on the frontier, almost always included a coat, a vest, a long-sleeved shirt, long pants and a hat. Men would rarely be seen in public without some type of coat and would remove it only in extreme heat and when there was no chance of encountering a woman in a social setting. Even in the forests and fields of No Man's Land, these social rules would have been followed by most of the settlers, at least those trying to move up the social ladder. Coats were usually made of linen for

Reproduction of typical male clothing on the frontier from the 1770s to the 1840s: hunting frock, straw hat, handmade sash and belt axe. *Photo by author.*

the summer and wool for the winter. Hunting frocks were popular work clothing for the woods and fields; they were cut to wrap around the body and often came to the knees of the wearer in order to protect the shirt, vest and pants from damage. From about 1800 to the 1830s, tailcoats with high collars were popular for social occasions. Over time, the height of the collars was reduced, and the frock coat replaced the tailcoat. Leather pants and shirts were common on the frontier, as buckskin was easier to acquire at times than cotton. However, few frontiersmen dressed only in buckskins, as most had a set of buckskin clothes and a set of cotton or wool clothing. Knee breeches had mostly fallen out of fashion by the beginning of the nineteenth century, replaced by long pants. The pants were narrow fall or broad fall, which means they had a flap in the front that could be opened. When button fly pants first came out, they were considered indecent, but by the 1840s, button flies were common.[114]

Until about age six, boys and girls wore similar outfits, often consisting of a long shirt coming below the knee. After age six, they started wearing smaller

Reproduction of a child's suit from the early 1840s. *Photo by author.*

versions of the clothes their parents wore, since there were no separate fashions for children and adults. Most clothes for children were hand-me-downs passed down from older sibling or refitted from their parents' clothes, often showing signs of many repairs and patches.[115]

Family life in American society in the nineteenth century was controlled by the father, who was seen as the head of the household in all matters, but the home was held together by the mother. There were very distinct tasks and social roles that men and women had at this time. A single or widowed woman could own property in her name; however, when she married, her legal identity was joined to that of her husband, and she could not own anything in her name. Men supervised most domestic matters, such as the rearing of children and hiring of household help, and had control over all the household finances, although women carried out most of the day-to-day activities of caring for the family and children. Payment for any work done outside of the home by women or children was given to the husband and recorded in account books under his name. Only men could vote in elections, hold public office or serve in the local militia. Even in most churches, women were not allowed to vote on church matters or become church officers.

The father may have been the head of the household, but the smooth operation of the home was the sphere of the mother and daughters. The wife took care of the children and oversaw their education, ensuring that members of the household were fed and clothed (which often included any hired hands as well) and doing other work that either provided an income or aided the smooth running of the home. The wife took great pride in her knowledge and skills in the culinary arts and use of the needle, loom and spinning wheel, and it was the mother's duty to pass these skills on to her daughters. It was common for women to help with harvests, but they normally did not work in the fields or forests unless there were unusual circumstances. Instead, women's daily work was centered on the home and included cooking meals over an open fire, planting and maintaining the kitchen garden and tending to the farmyard. Women tended to the chickens, collected the eggs, milked the cows, churned butter, pressed cheese, made soap and candles, gathered water from wells or springs, made and mended clothes and cleaned. All the while, the wife was busy making sure that the family would have enough food canned, salted, smoked, dried or preserved to make it through the winter without running out of food. When the temperatures turned cool enough, the process of butchering cattle, hogs and wild game began, and while the men did the heavy lifting and cutting, the women trimmed the meat into useable sizes and either salted or smoked the meat to preserve it.[116]

A far cry from the outlaw-run taverns like the Parker gang's Halfway House, several very nice hotels and taverns were opened along El Camino Real in the 1820s and 1830s. Sometime before 1826, John Baldwin, along with his wife and two daughters, opened a store, tavern, blacksmith shop and inn at a crossroads on the Texas Road about five miles west of Fort Jesup. The store was well stocked, as an 1826 advertisement in the *Natchitoches Courier* illustrates:[117]

Liqueurs—Madeira, Teneriff, Malaga, Claret wines, Cognac, Brandy, Holland and English Gins, West Indian Rum, Old and Common Whiskey
Coffee and Tea
Leaf lump and brown sugar
100 Sacks of salt
Boats, Shoes and Headwear
Cravats, Shawls, Collars and Cuffs (In Sets)

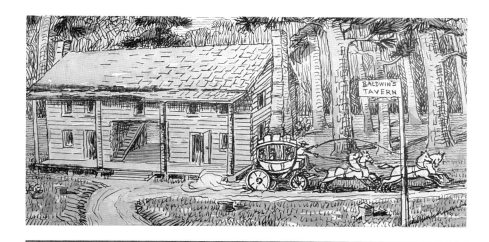

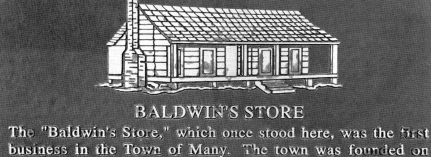

BALDWIN'S STORE

The "Baldwin's Store," which once stood here, was the first business in the Town of Many. The town was founded on May 17, 1843, when Judge W.R.D. Speight and others donated 40 acres to the newly-formed Sabine Parish Police Jury for the purpose of creating a parish seat. Baldwin's Store was built by John Baldwin and became the center of the town's government, as it served as a hotel, tavern, general mercantile, post office, city hall and courthouse. The store's architecture was that of a double pin, dog trot log house that was popular in that era.

Top: Artist's rendition of Baldwin's store. *By Amos Lee Armstong, from* Land of Green Gold *(Shreveport, LA: Jones and Stringfellow, 1958).*

Bottom: Historical marker for Baldwin's store, located near Hancock Whitney Bank in downtown Many, Louisiana. *Photo by author.*

Handkerchiefs and Lace, Belts, Ribbons and Buckles
Full and half cotton and wool hose
Mosquito bars
English gingham
Satins—black and blue
Bleached and unbleached cotton shirting
Modes de Fasion Chasimers, Fancy Calicoes
Superior friction-matches
Arm and Leg Garters
Medicines—½ bbl of hops, Jujube and Pectoral pastes, Swain's Panacea, Stillman's Sasparilla pills, Liverwort, Arrowroot, Horehound, Southern Cough drops, New England Cough Syrup, Oldridge's Balm-Columbia, Lavender Water and Rose Water
Ready to wear trousers and overcoats from $1.00 to $25.00
Tobacco for chewing and smoking. Extra sweet Havana cigars
Exquisite Organdies and Embroideries
Harness Buckles and Pistols
Also Suspenders and Corsets $1.00 each

Another pleasant hotel along the old El Camino Real was the Fort Jesup Hotel, which opened before 1837. In May 1837, A.W.P. Ursery ran an ad letting "his friends and the public" know that he "had taken the Fort Jesup Hotel and is now ready to receive company." Since its founding, Fort Jesup had been a social center, as officers and their wives hosted balls and moved in the social circles of both Natchitoches and, later, Sabine Parish. Concerts by the military bands were popular amusements, and Ursery played on their popularity in his advertisement, claiming that "the weary traveler will be regaled at night and morning by the delightful music of the well-known Military Band at the Fort, to listen to, which is a treat, which will doubtless be an inducement for many to call."[118]

One aspect that cannot be overlooked in the civilizing of No Man's Land is the role that churches played in community life. Not only did an increase in spiritual instruction soften the edges of this tough region, but the connections that the church provided would also lay the foundation to "civilize" the area. Aside from the more sacred aspect of attending a church service, these meetings provided many social connections. Over time, attendance expanded social networks beyond simple kin networks and connected families in a positive way. Congregations quickly learned that they could depend on each other in times of hardship and need. Churches also provided at least some basic informal education. Young people were able to meet and court in ways they would not have been able to without the regular central meetings. While one's denomination was important to these early settlers, for many, the specific church one attended was even more important. Many communities grew up near the church, and even today, many smaller communities take their name from the closest church.[119] While it would take several decades, starting in the 1840s and continuing through the twentieth century, the number of churches in No Man's Land would grow exponentially, and soon, even the smallest of communities would have several churches to meet the spiritual and social needs of people.

The first Protestant minister to preach west of the Mississippi River was the Reverend Joseph Willis, who would become the father of the Louisiana Baptist Convention. Joseph was born in Bladen County, North Carolina, in 1758. His father was Agerton Willis, and his mother, Sara, was a Native American slave. Joseph was the only son of Agerton and genuinely loved by his father. However, under North Carolina law, Joseph was born a slave. Not only were interracial marriages illegal, but North Carolina law also forbade slave owners from freeing slaves without the permission of the assembly. Despite his status, Agerton raised Joseph as a free person of color and left him a generous inheritance in his will. When Agerton died while Joseph was still a minor, the will was contested by Agerton's brother Daniel on the grounds that a slave could not own property, and Joseph lost the inheritance.[120]

During the American Revolution, Joseph joined Francis Marion's guerrilla force. Known as the Swamp Fox, Marion was famous for his hit-and-run tactics, which helped keep the British in South Carolina off balance. During this time, Joseph met two men who would have a lasting impact on his life. One was Ezekiel O'Quin, who would assist him in his missionary work, and the other was Richard Curtis Jr., who would eventually start the first Baptist church

Postcard of Fisher Baptist Church from the early 1900s. The congregation has built a new modern building on the site, and the original church has been moved to the historic square in Fisher. *Courtesy of United States Genealogy Web Project.*

in Mississippi. After the war, his cousin, John—the son of Joseph's uncle Daniel and a member of the North Carolina legislature—introduced a bill to restore Joseph's inheritance, which was approved. In 1798, Joseph sold his property and traveled to Mississippi with Curtis to help establish a church in Mississippi before traveling to Louisiana in 1799. At this time, Louisiana was still Spanish, and any religion other than Catholicism was illegal. From 1799 until the Louisiana Purchase, Joseph traveled the territory, holding meetings and planting churches at Plaquemine, Brule and Bayou Chicot, where he became known as the Apostle to the Opelousas. Willis was not as successful starting a church at Vermillion (modern-day Lafayette), where he was chased out of town for his preaching and moved on to Ville Platte. He next crossed into the southern part of No Man's Land and began establishing churches at Amiable, Occupy and Spring.[121]

When Willis applied for ordination from the Mississippi Baptist Association, there were some concerns over his dark skin and legal status as a "mulatto" (mixed White and Black ancestry), but the association voted to move forward with the ordination. In 1818, Willis helped start the Louisiana Baptist Association, and the five charter member churches were ones he had a hand in forming. As these churches grew, they sent missionaries out across the state to start new churches. It was also common for congregation members who moved into areas with no churches to start new ones in the community. Joseph Willis died in 1854 at his son's home at Oakdale, Louisiana, and is buried at Occupy Cemetery near Westport, Louisiana. Joseph funded much of his work by spending the money he made from the sale of his inheritance. He endured persecution, danger, the hardships of a frontier life and the death of three of his four wives, but he remained faithful to his calling. Most Louisiana churches founded before 1900 can trace their origins directly to Willis's missionary efforts or to the work of congregations he started. Many of these churches are still in existence today, serving their communities.[122]

As soon as the Louisiana Purchase was made, Methodist minsters entered Louisiana, and they soon began establishing churches. Often, these minsters were circuit riders attached to several churches who traveled from community to community to preach and conduct weddings, baptisms, funerals and revivals. It was often said of these pioneer pastors that they arrived at churches with a Bible in one hand and a gun in their saddlebag. Most depended on farming for their livelihood, as few churches paid their pastors at this time. One ceremonial duty that pastors were usually paid for was weddings. Young couples would frequently show up on the minister's

Oil painting of the first Aimwell Baptist Church building circa 1900. Members of one of the churches started by Joseph Willis moved into Sabine Parish in the 1890s and founded this church, which is still active today. *Courtesy of Aimwell Baptist Church.*

doorstep on a Saturday or Sunday afternoon and ask to be married, and after the ceremony, the couple would give the minister a gift for his services. If a young groom was inexperienced in the ways of the world and asked the minister how much the service would cost, the minster often replied something to the effect of, "How much is she worth to you?"[123]

As more Anglo Protestants moved into the region, the Catholic faith would further unite the Hispanic communities, with the church being one of their last cultural connections to their Spanish roots. However, even in a state that historically has had a very large Catholic population, these Hispanic Catholics were further isolated from the rest of Louisiana, whose church was heavily influenced by French language and culture and priests trained in France—whereas the Hispanic Catholic churches were influenced by the Spanish church, and their early priests were trained in seminaries in Spain or colonial Mexico until the early nineteenth century. Even today, the Catholic Church still plays a key social and cultural role in the remaining Hispanic communities.[124]

The Reverend and Mrs. Sherwood Jr. in a horse and buggy. Sherwood was a pastor in Sabine Parish in the early twentieth century. At the time of this picture, circa 1919, he was the pastor of Aimwell Baptist Church. *Courtesy of Aimwell Baptist Church.*

St. John the Baptist Catholic Church in Many, Louisiana. The church was founded in 1870, and when the building was renovated in the 1950s, the facade was designed in the Spanish Revival style to honor the Spanish heritage of Sabine Parish. *Photo by author.*

Daily life before the Civil War was difficult in No Man's Land, as settlers had to brave the dangers of outlaws and nature with limited manufactured goods, but those who chose to live there found a land that was rich in the resources they needed to farm, build houses and put food on the table. The land provided almost everything the settlers needed to live a simple yet, overall, happy life. They might not have had a lot of money, but there was food, shelter and family with little outside interference. Family and trusted friends provided a support network, and churches provided for both the spiritual and social needs of communities. Over time, better transportation and increased settlement allowed for more manufactured goods to be brought into No Man's Land, making life a little more comfortable. Although few in No Man's Land realized it, their lives—just as those of Americans across the country—would be changed forever with the coming of the Civil War.

CHAPTER 7

THE CHAOS OF THE CIVIL WAR AND RECONSTRUCTION

When the Civil War broke out in April 1861, it changed the country and No Man's Land forever. The settlers of the old Neutral Ground found themselves in the middle of national affairs when, for the most part, they just wanted to be left alone. Few in No Man's Land had strong feelings for or against slavery. Slavery was not a major part of the economy of No Man's Land, and there were only a small number of slave owners in the Sabine Strip. Except for a handful of large plantations, mostly in the northern part of the old Neutral Strip, most slave owners only owned a dozen slaves at most. The old Neutral Strip's location in the South did not automatically guarantee that its residents would be loyal to the Confederacy. While most of the early American settlers were from southern states, in the 1840s and 1850s, there was a small but steady increase in the number of settlers from northern states. Many Native Americans and Spanish and French descendants were unsure how to respond to the crisis. They had not been "American" long enough to have a deep sense of patriotism, and while some had felt mistreated by the United States, they were not sure how a new Southern nation would treat them. For all these reasons, the war was unpopular with many in No Man's Land. Soon, every family would have to choose where their loyalties lay. In the end, a large number of residents decided to join the Confederate army, and every region of No Man's Land raised volunteer units to join the Southern army. Those who did not support the Southern cause or the war in general had to decide what to do. Some left their homes and returned to the northern states they were from to join the Union army. Many tried to stay neutral, either attempting to continue their lives or taking to the swamps and woods to hide. Some chose their own self-interest, using the chaos and lack of police and military presence to start a new era of lawlessness, one that would rival the 1806–21 era for bloodshed and terror.

The Civil War made life very difficult for the civilian population left in No Man's Land, as most of the men went off to war, leaving women and young boys to try and run the farms. The Union blockade of Southern ports made it even more difficult to get manufactured goods in the area—by the end of the war, this was almost impossible. Adding to the confusion and hardships were bands of Union sympathizers, Southern draft dodgers and outlaws who banded together to form jayhawker groups. Most people think of the jayhawkers as only being from pre–Civil War Kansas, but the term came to be used throughout the South during the Civil War to describe the bands of outlaws that preyed on Confederate soldiers and civilians alike. While some did have strong pro-Union beliefs, most were just outlaws and draft dodgers who took advantage of the lack of law enforcement and absence of the men, who were off at the front, to raid and terrorize women and communities. Later in the war, they were able to prey on lightly defended Confederate supply trains moving out of Texas. As in the days before the 1819 treaty, there were few troops and few lawmen in the region between the Sabine and Calcasieu Rivers, and the area reverted to its lawless ways as it became a favorite target and hiding spot for jayhawkers and other criminals. By the end of the war, every parish in Louisiana had some level of jayhawker activity, with the highest amounts in the swamps west of the Mississippi, the marshlands of south Louisiana and the old No Man's Land. Bands of jayhawkers roamed the lands between the Sabine and Calcasieu, with the most activity in the areas around Hinston (Rapides Parish), Elizabeth (modern Allen Parish), Oberlin (modern Allen Parish) and Lake Charles. One of the larger groups that operated in the old Neutral Strip was the Mermentau Jayhawkers, which numbered over two hundred mounted men who stole cattle and sold them to Union forces. The Sabine Jayhawkers used the Bear Head Creek area (modern Calcasieu and Beauregard Parish), the Calcasieu Jayhawkers roamed the bottomlands of the Calcasieu River and the Beckwith Jayhawkers were located on the eastern side of the Calcasieu River.[125] Not everyone who hid out during the war became a jayhawker. Some of the descendants of Spanish and Native American settlers did not feel that they were part of American society, let alone Southern society, due to their treatment by Whites, so they hid to avoid fighting for either

Reproduction Enfield rifle-musket, which was used by both sides during the Civil War. *Photo by author.*

side. These men hid in the Sabine River bottom to avoid recruiting officers. Oral histories from the Zwolle-Ebarb area relate stories of men who were discovered by officials and carried off against their will to fight in the Civil War and were never seen again. Not everyone from these communities chose not to fight, as there were several men from Spanish and Native American communities who did fight in the Southern army.[126]

Cattle rustling continued to be a common crime along the Sabine during the Civil War and the post–Civil War era. While West Texas is famous for its cattle drives, large cattle drives through the former Neutral Strip were common decades before Texas drives. However, not all the cattle drives in the former Neutral Strip were done by the legal owners of the herds. One gang that was famous for driving herds of stolen cattle was led by the McGee family, who lived a few miles north of Newton, Texas. Sometimes they would steal cattle in Texas and drive them across the Sabine to Louisiana to sell, but most often, they stole the cattle in Louisiana and drove them to Texas. The McGees and their gang had a unique moral code, in that they never robbed people of money or goods and did not steal horses. According to local lore, if the McGees borrowed something, they returned double the amount borrowed. However, murder to cover their tracks and cattle stealing were considered acceptable under their code.[127]

The McGees went too far one day when they ambushed and killed Charles and Claiborne Hart to keep them from informing the authorities of their cattle stealing. The ambush happened in Louisiana on the Spikes family property, which later became Whitman's Ferry. When word of the murders reached the town of Newton, about fifty citizens rode out, crossed the Sabine River and captured several family members and their gang. They were taken back to Newton, where two of the ringleaders, Bowie McGee and Benton Wibum, were shot. Some gang members escaped and continued to cause trouble on both sides of the Sabine River until after the Civil War. Big Bud and Little Bud, brothers of the late Bowie McGee, hid in the former Neutral Strip to avoid service in the Civil War, becoming jayhawkers and stealing to survive. Both brothers would die of pneumonia before the end of the war. After the war, other members of the gang continued to terrorize their neighbors, until another group of citizens had enough and ambushed the gang while they were branding cattle. A Mr. Hassell, who had married a McGee girl, was killed; three of the McGee girls were killed; and the matriarch of the family, "Aunt Polly," was wounded. After the ambush, many of the McGees moved to West Texas, where Bill McGee (Bowie McGee's brother) was murdered.[128]

Reconstruction in the South was a terrifying time of lawlessness, economic depression and racial tension. Random acts of violence were common throughout the South. One case of this random violence happened in December 1876 when the Horton gang, who had been terrorizing East Texas for years, crossed the Sabine River and rode into Natchitoches. On Christmas Day, they began shooting and terrorizing any African Americans they could find. Local citizens fought back, and several members of the Horton gang were killed, including some of the leaders; the rest fled back through the old No Man's Land back to East Texas.[129]

During this time, not even being a lawman was a guarantee of safety, as Seth Smith would soon find out when he crossed the Stephens family. Tom Stephens was born in Alabama in 1828 and moved to Louisiana in 1857. In 1860, Tom was living as a farmer in a part of Rapides Parish that would later become Vernon Parish, and when the Civil War broke out, he joined Company K, Sixth Louisiana Cavalry. After the war, Tom settled on Ten Mile Creek and lived there until 1874, when he sold his property. Next, Tom lived for a time in Calcasieu Parish, later moving to the Sabine River in Vernon Parish, near the Evans/Burr Ferry area. Tom Stephens was a large, powerful man weighing around three hundred pounds. His wife, Epsey, was six feet tall and, from all reports, a beautiful woman. The couple had several children, including Margaret, Ann, Rebecca, Robert Preston, George Thomas, Sherman J., John C. and Sheridan (often spelled "Sheradan").[130] Tom was a known gambler who had a room added to his house for gambling and was known to have killed several men.

According to family lore, Epsey was pampered by her family. She had two servants and had been given a large dog which stayed at her side. One day, Seth Smith, who was a lawman and may have been a federal officer, came to the house. As he was approaching Epsey, the dog started growling at him, and Seth kicked the dog. According to family history, Epsey told Seth not to kick the dog again, and Smith "called her an ugly word and told her he would kick her." Their son Robert Preston, who was a teenager, heard what Seth said and swore to teach him a lesson. Several years later, Robert, who by this time had a wife and children, heard that Smith was coming back to the area on the riverboat *Fountain*. Robert went to the dock and shot Seth Smith when he got off the boat. From that time forward, the Stephens family and their friends banded together to prevent Robert's capture. Law enforcement officials vowed to bring Robert to justice and were aided by local citizens, but the Stephens family seemed to be one step ahead of them, due to their large family and kin network. There were many ambushes and armed raids, but the Stephenses were always able to shoot their way out or avoid the trap. The violence continued for several years, and many people on both sides were killed.[131]

Sometime around 1881, Tom and a friend named Hinson were taken by surprise and captured. They were told they were going to be taken to Lake Charles, where the pair assumed they would be killed. On the way, they stopped overnight, and Tom and Hinson were locked in a building under guard. Hinson began crying, convinced they would soon be killed, but Tom realized that there was already a gap between the dirt floor and the wall. When Hinson saw Tom was digging a hole, believing that they might really be able to escape, he stopped crying. Tom told him to keep crying so the guard would not become suspicious. The pair slipped under the wall and made it back to Tom's house. After the close call, Tom started hiding out at a camp about five miles from his home. Each day, Epsey would bring him food and supplies. One day in 1881, while Epsey was there, the state militia raided the camp without warning. Tom was killed in the gunfight, and Epsey was hit in the hip by a stray bullet. Tom is buried in the Cooper Cemetery near Pickering, Louisiana. According to legend, Tom killed twenty-one men in twenty-one years and said, "If I live another 21 years I'll kill 21 more."[132]

Many other members of the Stephens family also met violent ends. Robert was killed in 1896 near Shoats Creek in a feud with the Foster family over the boat landing at Nibblet's Bluff. George was killed in a dance hall fight. Sheridan killed his brother Wesley, who apparently had been bullying him for years. Sheridan would die of pneumonia in the early 1900s, alone and destitute. He was buried in an unmarked grave in the Science Hill Cemetery near Glenmora, Louisiana; his only possession was a small pocket watch, known at the time as a "dollar watch."[133]

Sometimes, former criminals went to great lengths to hide their identities so that their past crimes would not be found out, but few went as far as Bill Longley. Longley had fled Texas after committing a murder and settled in the northern part of the old Neutral Strip. He became a farmer and led a crime-free life. Longley even went so far as to help local lawmen apprehend criminals when extra men were needed. Unfortunately for Longley, his past caught up with him, and he was apprehended by a group of Texas and Louisiana lawmen near Keatchie in DeSoto Parish in 1877. Longley was taken to Giddings, Texas, where he was found guilty and hanged.[134]

For most of the nineteenth century, the area of No Man's Land was thinly populated, and with few roads, most of the region was inaccessible. But starting in the late nineteenth century and increasing exponentially in the early twentieth century, the impassable ancient forests would become the main economic resource, combined with the railroad, that would lead to the settlement of much of the old Neutral Strip. The lumber companies built not only mills throughout western Louisiana but also towns, churches, schools, doctor's offices and stores, and in the twentieth century, electricity and ice were brought to areas that had only dreamed of such luxuries. The roads and railroads that the lumber companies built connected the region of No Man's Land with the rest of the United States in ways it had never been connected before.

Early logging camp. *Courtesy Vernon Parish History.*

This newfound wealth and prosperity of the timber industry were not without issues. Some were the typical problems of early American industry. With few laws to protect workers, some of the companies took advantage of them. Lumber mills were difficult, dangerous places to work, and employees often worked long hours cutting trees, transporting them to the mill and then sawing the logs into lumber, all with primitive safety standards. Company leaders were involved in local politics and, because of their economic impact, often had the support of local politicians and law enforcement. Some of the companies only paid in company script (basically a certificate or paper money issued by the company) that could only be used at company stores. Sometimes the companies would change the form of their script, invalidating older script and making any savings the workers had worthless. The lumber mills and supporting operations created so many jobs that there were not enough local people to fill them.[135] So, in an area where mistrust of outsiders was commonplace, you now had thousands of outsiders from all parts of America and immigrants from around the world. Tensions between all these outsiders and those who were already there increased, intensifying mistrust and reinforcing the clannish nature of No Man's Landers.

As tensions between workers and company owners also increased, workers began turning to unions to try and improve conditions. At this time, unions had no legal standing, and unions and strikes were often broken by force as strikebreakers (hired thugs and gunmen) threatened workers and attacked or murdered union members. One such effort to unionize was led by Arthur L. Emerson, a former millwright, who started the Brotherhood of Timber Workers at Fullerton and began trying to start unions in mills throughout Louisiana and East Texas in 1910. In 1912, efforts to unionize the Grabow Mill near Merryville in Beauregard Parish would soon lead to the Grabow Riot and the legend of Leather Britches Smith.[136]

Almost nothing is known of Charles "Leather Britches" Smith before he arrived in Merryville. Most believed he was from Texas, and many thought that he was fleeing from a murder charge. Some thought he was crazy, while others thought that he was only half crazy, but everyone agreed he was an expert marksman able to shoot birds from the sky left- or right-handed with both rifle and pistol. Leather Britches was not a man to be taken lightly, and most tried to avoid him.[137]

When Emerson and the Brotherhood of Timber Workers' demands that workers at Grabow be paid every two weeks were rejected, plans were made for a strike. On July 7, 1912, Leather Britches Smith, along with many workers and townspeople, attended a pro-union rally where Emerson was to be the keynote speaker. Although reports varied, most agree that during the meeting, mill owners, company men and hired guns opened fire on the crowd, most of whom were unarmed. One who was not unarmed was Leather Britches Smith, who began returning fire; soon, other union men joined in the gunfight. Several men were killed before the shooting stopped. Not long after the smoke cleared, arrests were made, but since the mill owners had the support of local law enforcement, only union men were arrested. A total of sixty union men were arrested, but not a single company man was arrested. The union men were not charged with the death of the company men but, instead, for the death of Decatur Hall, himself a union man. Only nine of the sixty were bought to trial, and all nine were acquitted. One man who was not arrested was Leather Britches Smith; instead, he was ambushed a few weeks after the riot while he walked on a stretch of railroad tracks near Merryville and was killed.[138]

The lumber industry would bring an increase in population throughout No Man's Land, but as with many other parishes in the region, Sabine Parish would see many difficulties between the established residents and the newcomers. Because of this, the area around Zwolle and Ebarb would gain a reputation for being a tough place. These communities were already at odds with their Anglo neighbors, as they were historically and culturally Spanish (though often mistaken for Mexican), were Catholic instead of Protestant, spoke an archaic Spanish dialect and had intermarried with Native Americans—and because of these differences, they endured a great deal of racism. Fights between residents were common and were often fueled by racism and misunderstandings between earlier settlers and newcomers. Often, the Hispanic residents felt they had no choice but to fight, and sometimes they fought back simply to show that that they could. It's no wonder that the area would earn a "notorious reputation" with outsiders.[139]

The modern town of Zwolle would be founded in 1896 as a lumber town when the Kansas City Southern (KCS) railroad put in a line about a mile north of Bayou Scie. Many of the descendants of the Spanish settlers relocated to the new town, which was named by a Dutch railroad investor for his hometown of Zwolle in the Netherlands. This put the Hispanic descendants in conflict with other settlers coming into the area for jobs with the lumber mills and railroads. In the late nineteenth and early twentieth centuries, being Spanish or Indian was seen as a "social handicap." Many prominent community members or those who wanted to elevate their social position were likely to discourage or even forbid their children from speaking Spanish or Native languages, and many last names were changed to erase evidence of Spanish descent. For example, in the northern part of Sabine Parish, names such as Bermea were changed to Malmay, Ybarbo to Ebarb, Garcia to Garcie, del Rio to Rivers and Parrilla to Parrie. Just as southern Louisiana had a "no French" policy in schools, there was also a "no Spanish" policy in Hispanic areas, so there was no speaking of Spanish in schools. Because of this policy, sometimes last names were changed by teachers—for example, Sharneca to Ezernack. Often, older residents would not speak Spanish around school-age children for fear that it would "mess up their little minds."[140]

Life remained hard in No Man's Land throughout the early twentieth century, but with the coming of the railroads and lumber mills, and the increases in technology and population, life slowly became a little easier. But even these advances brought new problems, as they brought older settlers into conflict with newcomers, and newcomers often looked down on the cultures of older settlers. Boys learned at a young age to fight their own battles, and this willingness to fight and mistrust of outsiders carried through to adulthood. The territory may have become part of the United States in 1821, but it would take until well after World War II before the people fully became part of Louisiana and American society, while at the same time holding on to the traditions and folkways that had helped them survive No Man's Land.

CHAPTER 8

BECOMING AMERICAN

THE LASTING LEGACY OF NO MAN'S LAND

Officially, the Neutral Strip Agreement lasted less than twenty years, but the impact of No Man's Land can still be felt in the twenty-first century. Because the region was not open to legal settlement as early as the rest of Louisiana, it was sparsely populated until the early twentieth century, when the arrival of the railroad would lead to the birth of the lumber and forestry industries in western Louisiana. The area of the Neutral Strip has always been a border region: first between Native American groups, then between the Spanish and the French, next between Spain and the United States, later between the United States and Mexico, then between the United States and the Republic of Texas and now between Louisiana and Texas. The physical separation caused by the distance between settlers of the region and centers of government has led to the feeling that they are on their own. Often, the self-sufficiency needed to survive in a border region leads to a mistrust of government and outsiders. Many settlers took the attitude that if you are not sure who is a friend or foe, it is easier to trust only your friends and family.

When the Neutral Ground was officially added to the United States, there were only small pockets of settlers scattered throughout the region. Instead of dividing the Neutral Strip into parishes, the land was simply added to the closest parish. There were three western Louisiana parishes in 1821—Natchitoches covered most of northwest Louisiana, Rapides was in the middle and St. Landry covered all of southwestern Louisiana—so the boundaries of these parishes were simply extended to the Sabine River. Although it would still take decades for No Man's Land to become civilized, starting in the 1820s, large numbers of settlers came pouring into western Louisiana, and within two decades, the population was large enough to begin dividing the region into parishes. The process would begin in the 1840s and would not be completed until the twentieth century, but as with everything in No Man's Land, this process was not always smooth and often made tensions between old and new settlers flare up again.

Imperial Calcasieu Parish was the first of the No Man's Land parishes to be created. On August 24, 1840, representatives from the six western wards met to establish a new parish, which would be created out of the western part of St. Landry Parish. One of the main reasons for this separation was the time it took to travel. For early settlers of Calcasieu, it could take six or seven days one way to travel to the parish seat of St. Landry Parish at Opelousas. Since there were no public buildings in that part of the parish, the meeting was held at the rough-hewn home of Arsene LeBleu near present-day Chloe. The first jurymen who assembled that day were David Simmons, Alexander Hebert, Michel Pithon, Henry Moss, Rees Perkins and Thomas M. Williams. They first elected officers and a parish clerk and decided on a set of simple parliamentary rules that would give the jury president authority to keep their meetings orderly and progressive. Their first major deliberation was about establishing the parish seat. Locations nominated were Lisbon (west of the Calcasieu River), Comasaque Bluff (east of the river, later called Marsh Bayou Bluff), Centre (in the center of the parish) and Faulk's Bluff (a point of land above Joseph Faulk's place). Comasaque Bluff, which was a crossroads and a ferry crossing, was selected after the jury president voted to break a tie between it and Lisbon. On December 8, 1840, it was resolved that the seat of justice be given the name of Marion.[141]

In 1843, the Louisiana legislature authorized the people to vote on the question of moving the parish seat, but no change was made at that time. In 1852, Jacob Ryan pushed to move the seat of justice from Marion to the east bank of Lake Charles. In large part, this move was because of the rising connection between the lumber industries around Lake Charles and Galveston, Texas. Businessman Jacob Ryan and lawyer Samuel Kirby felt that the courthouse at Marion was too remote to effectively take care of legal matters, so they pushed for the seat of government to be moved to the eastern shore of Lake Charles. Instead of building a courthouse, the courthouse of Marion was rolled to the river, loaded on a barge and transported twelve miles downriver, where it was unloaded and rolled to a spot of land near where the current courthouse is today. This parish seat was incorporated in 1857 as Charleston, but due to the unpopularity of that name, it was

Four Lake Charles policemen circa 1890. *Standing, left to right*: Charles Clerc and Shelby Gauthier, chief. *Seated, left to right*: George A. Miller and Ira Barker. *McNeese State University Archives.*

reincorporated in 1868 as Lake Charles. It is located about six miles from the original parish seat of Marion, which is now known as Old Town.[142]

Sabine Parish would be created in 1843 from part of Natchitoches Parish, although the original boundaries would be larger than those of the modern parish. Much of the early Anglo settlement of the parish was along the two major roads running through the parish, the San Antonio Trace (old El Camino Real) and Nolan's Trace. The most populated area in the parish was near Fort Jesup, and there was discussion of making Fort Jesup the parish seat, but it was decided that since it was an active military post and not being centrally located, the parish government would need to be housed somewhere else.

It was decided that a location near Baldwin's Store, which was centric and at a crossroads with the San Antonio Trace and many other roads, would be ideal. Baldwin donated some of the land near his store for a town plot, the lots were sold to raise money for public buildings and the new town was named Many in honor of James B. Many, who had been the post commander at Fort Jesup for almost fourteen years. One of the first areas in Sabine Parish to be settled was the area around Negreet Bayou in 1822, by Christopher Anthony; by 1826, there was a large enough population that Zion Hill Baptist Church was organized. The Toro Creek area was settled by William Curtis and John McCollister in the early 1820s; by 1827, there were enough settlers to found Pleasant Hill Church, and in 1848, Toro Baptist Church was organized. Soon, the Toro Creek community became known as Pleasant Hill, not to be confused with the Pleasant Hill community in northern Sabine Parish, which would be founded decades later. When the post office opened in the community in the early twentieth century, it was named Toro, because there was already a Pleasant Hill post office in northern Sabine Parish, and the community was again known as Toro.[143]

Like all parishes of the old No Man's Land, the railroad and the lumber industry would bring population growth and the birth of many new communities to Sabine Parish. Before 1885, merchants of the towns of Fort

Top: Downtown Many, November 1904. *Courtesy of United States Genealogy Web Project.*

Bottom: Bank of Zwolle, early 1900s. *Courtesy of United States Genealogy Web Project.*

Jesup and Many had their goods shipped from New Orleans by Red River steamboats to Grand Ecore, near Natchitoches, then transported them by wagon to their stores. In 1885, the Texas Pacific Railroad extended a line to Robeline, meaning that goods could now be delivered by rail and picked up in Robeline, shortening both the time it took to receive an order and the wagon trip to pick it up. It would not be until 1896 that Sabine Parish received a railroad, which was built by the Kansas City Southern Railway, providing direct freight transportation and improving mail service. This was a blessing for the town of Many, as the rail line went through the parish seat instead of through Fort Jesup, which was still the largest population center even though it was no longer a military post, leading to an economic and population boom for Many and the slow decline of Fort Jesup as people and businesses moved to Many to be closer to the railroad. Pleasant Hill, in the northern part of Sabine Parish, started out in DeSoto Parish around 1840, but when the Texas Pacific Railroad built a line south of the village, the village voted to move to the railroad. The village government relocated to the rail line, and most of the village was now in Sabine Parish. The village of Noble was first settled around 1830 but saw population growth in 1896 when the KCS railroad built a line close to the village. The town of Zwolle was established in 1896 when the KCS line was constructed. There has been a lumber mill on the site of the current Weyerhaeuser Mill for over one hundred years, and in the early twentieth century, there was a great deal of oil field activity in the region. Many of the descendants of the early Spanish settlers who lived close to the town moved a few miles to the town center to be closer to job opportunities at the mill and oil field, leading to altercations and difficulties with the newcomers in the town. Converse, in the northern part of Sabine Parish, was founded in 1906 along the KCS line and named for Colonel James Converse, who owned a large tract of land near the town site. Fisher, five miles south of Many, was the first major sawmill town in Sabine Parish, founded in 1899 by the Louisiana Long Leaf Lumber Company (4L Co.) as a company town, meaning the lumber company owned and built all the homes and other buildings, then rented them to employees. Unlike many other early lumber companies, the Long Leaf company did not use clear-cutting to collect timber but instead practiced an early form of land management, allowing it to stay in business many years after most of the other lumber mills in the region had closed because they no longer had trees to cut near the mills. Although the mill at Fisher closed in the 1960s, many of the village buildings have been preserved and are listed in the National Register of Historic Places. The town of Florien, located twelve miles south of Many along the KCS line, was founded in 1896 and was named for Florien Giauque, a permanent lawyer in Cincinnati, Ohio, who took an interest in land in Sabine Parish and, in 1879, started buying thousands of acres in the parish. Eventually, Florien would build a large lumber mill, which is now owned by Boise Cascade.[144]

Settlers were in the region that was to become DeSoto Parish before the Louisiana Purchase, with the largest area of population being the French settlement at Bayou Pierre. With the opening of the Red River to steamboat travel in early 1830s, large numbers of cotton farmers from the Carolinas, Georgia, Alabama and Mississippi began settling in the northern section of the future parish. In 1843, DeSoto Parish would be created out of part of Natchitoches and Caddo Parish, with a land mass of 876 square miles. The first meeting of parish officers was held at Screamerville, two miles west of where Grand Cane would be founded. The first officers were John E. Hewitt, John Wagoner, Simeon De Soto, J.A. Gamble and C.A. Edwards.

Left: Original steam whistle from the Fisher Sawmill, now on display at the Louisiana History Museum in Alexandria, Louisiana. *Photo by author.*

Below: 4L (Louisiana Long Leaf Lumber) Company Store building built circa 1900 in Fisher, Louisiana. This building, along with several others, is still standing in the town square. *Photo by author.*

During 1843, the police jury met several times at Screamerville, using the store of Crosby and Carruth, which was owned by William Crosby and John Carruth. The issue of where the parish seat would be soon become a major point of contention between the descendants of French settlers and the newer American settlers. The settlers at Bayou Pierre wanted the parish seat to be Old Augusta, while the cotton farmers and newer American settlers wanted it to be Screamerville. A compromise was finally reached, whereby a new town would be formed halfway between each community to serve as the parish seat. Town plots for the new village of Mansfield were laid out, and a log courthouse was completed on August 4, 1843, which would serve the parish until 1853. One of the historic events that took place at the courthouse was a ball for the volunteers organized from DeSoto Parish before they left for the Mexican War in 1846. Mansfield would officially be incorporated in 1847. The first post office in DeSoto Parish was at Screamerville and was in the home of Maria Davidson; the mail was delivered twice a week. Logansport was founded in 1830 by Dr. Logan, who practiced medicine on both sides of the Sabine River and operated a ferry. He originally called his settlement Waterloo, but over time, the name changed first to Logan's Ferry and finally to Logansport. The town saw tremendous growth when the Houston and Shreveport Railroad built a line through it in 1885. Grand Cane was founded in 1882 along the Texas Pacific Railroad line.[145]

Cameron Parish was created out of parts of Calcasieu and Vermilion Parishes in 1870 and named for Simon Cameron, who was Abraham Lincoln's secretary of war until 1862. Today, Cameron Parish is the largest of the Louisiana parishes but has the lowest population in the state, for many reasons. The earliest people to live in the parish were the Atakapa, and their presence limited early European settlement. With the Louisiana Purchase, Cameron was included in the Neutral Ground agreement, and settlement was illegal. Just as in other parts of No Man's Land, the outlaws poured in, and the marshland and coastlines made convenient hideouts for smugglers such as Jean and Pierre Lafitte. Tradition tells us that the first White settlers in the area were a family bearing the surname of Phillips. They lived at the western end of Grand Chenier beside the bank of the Mermentau in a shack built of poles covered with palmettos. A lone Indian had attached himself to their household. A hurricane swept in, possibly in 1824, and killed the family; the sole survivor was the Indian. He later crossed the marshes until he found other settlers, to whom he reported the tragedy. After the Sabine River was set as the boundary, the federal government sent in officials to control the territory, but unlike in other parts of No Man's Land, the

Left: Historic DeSoto Parish Courthouse. *Courtesy of the DeSoto Chamber of Commerce.*

Below: Downtown Logansport in the early twentieth century. *Courtesy of the DeSoto Chamber of Commerce.*

government heavily limited settlement in the area of present-day Cameron until the 1830s. Congress reserved the large tracts of live oak forestland as naval reserves, to provide lumber to build wooden sailing vessels for the navy. By the 1830s, it was determined that such vast amounts of oak timber were no longer needed for shipbuilding, and an amendment was passed to free the cheniers (oak groves) for private ownership in Cameron and other parts of the United States. As part of the bill to open the oak groves, Congress passed a law to pay many elderly army veterans with land grants to the formerly reserved naval lands. However, many of the elderly or middle-aged veterans had little desire to move westward, so they sold their grants to speculators, who in turn sold to prospective landowners. These landowners soon came into conflict with the squatters who had been living on the land without titles for years. In the 1830s and '40s, a wave of migration from Virginia, the Carolinas, Georgia, Alabama and Mississippi swept into the cheniers. Later, descendants of the displaced Acadians or of French Creoles settled in the region. Early census records contain names of individuals born in various foreign countries who settled in the parish.[146]

Vernon Parish was created on March 30, 1871, out of parts of Sabine, Rapides and Natchitoches Parishes. Very little historical documentation relating to the founding of the parish has survived, so a great deal of the information surrounding it has been preserved as folklore and oral history. Even the origin of the name of the parish has been lost. Some say it was named after the house that George Washington lived in, called Mount Vernon; some say it was named after either a famous racehorse named Vernon or a mule named Vernon; and some believe it was named for Vernon, Ohio, where several of the early settlers were from. What is known is that Vernon Parish owes its existence to Senator John R. Smart. Smart, who was a senator from Sabine Parish, pushed for a bill to create the parish and laid out its boundaries. The northern boundary does not run in a straight line from the eastern boundary to the Sabine River, and as a result of how the boundaries were drawn, three of Smart's political rivals (Lucius, Nash and Presley) were left in Sabine Parish. The act also stipulated that the parish seat was to be located on or near Bayou Castor. This land belonged to Dr. Edmund Ellison Smart, who had his doctor's office and co-owned a general store on the property. Dr. Smart was the son of Senator Smart. The first police jury meeting was held in Smart's doctor's office. Soon, Smart donated eighty acres of land for the parish seat and courthouse, located where the current courthouse now stands. He named the town Leesville. On August 14, 1871, the police jury opened sealed bids for the construction of a courthouse. The building was a two-story pine log structure measuring fifty by one hundred feet and cost $4,250 to build. The bid was awarded to John F. Smart, who was not a son of Senator Smart but likely related to him.[147]

There were probably three to four thousand people in Vernon Parish when it was created. By 1890, the population had only increased by about 14 percent, but by 1900, it had grown by 75 percent, due to the lumber industry. By the early twentieth century, there were dozens of new towns in Vernon Parish due to the lumber industry and the railroads. However, by the 1930s, most of these villages were nothing more than a memory. A few towns survived after the lumber industry left and are still active, although smaller than their boom times. The Anacoco Post Office was

Opposite, top left: Mitchell and Lola Hinson. *Courtesy of Vernon Parish History.*

Opposite, top right: Nelie Steele Wiley. *Courtesy of Vernon Parish History.*

Opposite, bottom left: William and Sarah Knight Walters. *Courtesy of Vernon Parish History.*

Opposite, bottom right: Vernon Parish deputies around the turn of the twentieth century. *Bottom left*: Walsh McRae. *Top middle*: Bill Turner. Others are not identified. *Courtesy of Vernon Parish History.*

Above: Tavern at Burr's Ferry around the turn of the twentieth century. *Courtesy of Vernon Parish History.*

first opened in 1855, closed in 1866, then reopened in 1875. The area around Hornbeck was settled in the 1830s but would not become a town until 1897. F.A. Hornbeck divided the land into a town plat and began selling lots when it was confirmed the railway was coming. Rosepine was laid out in 1896 by Wyatt Herrington, who had received forty acres from Thomas Evans. Anacoco was a thriving town between 1871 to 1897 due to its location on the main road running south from Many and was a popular stop for travelers. The town grew even faster in 1897, once the railroad came through, but it, like most of the parish, saw a decline in population after the lumber mills closed. The beginning of World War II saw a huge increase in the parish population, as the region was used for major war games and troop training. Camp Polk was established in 1940, and by the end of the war, over eight million men had passed through the post for training before being deployed. The camp was renamed Fort Polk in 1955

Charlie and Martha Swain's homestead on Six Mile Creek in Vernon Parish. *Courtesy of the Museum of West Louisiana.*

and is still a major training center for the United States Army as well as being at the heart of the Vernon Parish economy. The designation of the post was changed to Fort Johnson in 2023.[148]

Two of the last three of the modern sixty-four parishes to be created were in the former No Man's Land. Beauregard and Allen Parishes had similar settlement patterns to the other Neutral Ground regions, but because of their dense forests and the lack of major trade routes through the parishes, there was little to attract early Spanish or French settlers. When Louisiana was ceded to Spain in 1763, the Crown tried to attract settlers to the region by offering a square league of land, along with provisions, farming implements and cattle. While this helped attract some settlers—including a few French, Spanish and English and even some Acadians—the area was still sparsely populated at the time of the Louisiana Purchase. Many of the French and Acadians settled in the southern part of modern Allen Parish, where they found a large prairie east of the Calcasieu River suitable for rice farming. The Anglo-Saxon American settlers (from South Carolina, Georgia, Mississippi and Florida) preferred the wooded areas of modern northern Allen Parish and Beauregard Parish and began arriving after 1816.

The first American settler in the area of present-day Beauregard Parish was "Saddler" Johnson, who earned his nickname due to his skills as a saddlemaker. He settled in what would become the Sugartown community. Other early settlers were Edwards Eacoubas, Dempsey Iles, John L. Lyons, Joseph W. Moore, E. Sherley, James Simmons, William B. Welborn, Ezra Young and G.W. Corkran. The second community was that of Dry Creek, founded by Thomas W. Williams. Another settlement was founded

Steamboat *Neches Bell*, which
traveled the Sabine River
in the late 1800s through
the early 1900s. *Courtesy of
Vernon Parish History.*

at Petersburg in the late 1830s or early 1840s. It was named after Pete
Eddleman, one of the settlers. Most of the residents of this settlement came
from South Carolina and Florida. The Calcasieu area received an influx of
people from Hancock County, Mississippi, between 1848 and 1851, and a
number of them settled in present-day Beauregard Parish. During the next
decade, the area was settled rapidly, and it has been estimated that the area
that is now Beauregard Parish contained a population of four thousand.
During the Civil War, a portion of this group migrated to the North, as they
did not support secession from the Union.[149]

Sugartown was the first settlement in what would become Beauregard
Parish and was settled around 1816. The town also holds the honor of
having the first cotton gin in the parish and the first school, Sugartown Male
and Female Academy, which opened in 1879 and ran for two years before
it closed. Dry Creek and Big Woods were founded soon after Sugartown.
In 2023, Sugartown had a population of about 154 residents. Like so many
other parts of No Man's Land, the major population boom came with the
railroad and the lumber mills. DeRidder, Merryville and Longville all started
as mill towns.[150]

The major settlement of Allen Parish began with the establishment
of Kinder and Oakdale after the Kansas City and Gulf Railway was
constructed through the region. Oberlin was settled by residents of
Oberlin, Ohio, whose original plan was to create a college town. The
town of Elizabeth started as a lumber town. Like most of No Man's Land,
Allen Parish had a small population before the lumber industry arrived.
During the Civil War, the large stands of timber made excellent hideouts

for jayhawkers, and many large groups of jayhawkers used the region as a base of operations.

When the Neutral Ground was added to the United States, the southern part was added to St. Landry Parish; later, these lands would become Imperial Calcasieu Parish. Cameron Parish was the first parish carved out of Imperial Calcasieu, in 1870, but even with the loss of Cameron, from 1870 until 1912, Imperial Calcasieu was still the largest parish in Louisiana, covering an area of about 3,600 square miles. In 1908, a group of businessmen from DeRidder, Sugartown and Merryville had a bill drawn up to create a parish, but the bill was voted down. In June 1911, a meeting was held at Oakdale to discuss restarting the effort to separate the large parish into several smaller parishes. This was followed by a meeting at Lake Charles attended by representatives from various parts of the parish, and at this meeting, it was agreed to divide the parish. After an October 1911 meeting to elect delegates, the delegates met to draw up boundary lines for the new parishes. This committee presented its report to the state legislature in May 1912, and the parishes of Jefferson Davis, Allen and Beauregard were created.[151]

Like much of No Man's Land, both Beauregard and Allen Parishes showed a population increase of 25 to 50 percent between 1910 and 1920 due to the timber industry, which hit its peak between 1915 and 1920. However, after 1920, when much of the timberland had been cut, the population started a steep decline. By 1930, Beauregard had lost almost 30 percent of its population. By the 1940s, many of the parishes of No Man's Land saw a gradual increase in population, as farmers began taking advantage of all the cleared land to grow crops and raise cattle.[152]

Treasure hunting would become a popular activity in No Man's Land, helping to preserve many of the stories and legends of outlaws and jayhawkers well into the twentieth century. There were two types of jayhawker treasure: loot they had stolen and treasure that people hid to keep them out of the jayhawkers' hands. In modern Calcasieu Parish, a jayhawker campground near Edgerly has been a popular treasure-hunting spot, as rumors of buried loot are still spread even today. Modern Allen Parish is also full of jayhawker treasure stories. One is of a group of jayhawkers who jumped a detachment of Confederate troops near Elizabeth and captured about $40,000 in goods and treasure—but, at least according to the legend, were forced to bury their loot and were unable to recover it. In the southern part of No Man's Land, many stories involve "jayhawker money," money and other valuables buried by families to keep them out of the jayhawkers' hands. After the war, the families were either unable to return to receive their goods or unable to find them when they tried. Even as late as the 1940s, searching for jayhawker money was a common pastime. Many treasure stories also have a supernatural element, as many of the treasures were supposed to be cursed to protect them. According to legend, many of Jean Lafitte's treasures are guarded by the ghost of a slave or crewmember who was killed and buried with the treasure to guard it for eternity or until Lafitte returned and released the spirit to the afterlife.[153]

These treasure stories have also helped preserve the memory of many sites where settlers camped, as these campsites became popular spots to search. Fallen Springs, about four miles south of the town of Many, which had been a favorite campsite for travelers, later became a popular treasure-hunting site. Legends were rampant about travelers who buried gold there to hide it from outlaws and were unable to find it or were killed before they returned to it, with even more stories of outlaws who buried gold and treasure to make a fast escape but were unable to return to the site. As to the success of these treasurer hunters, one early Sabine Parish historian wrote in 1912, "If any man has recovered an amount sufficient to pay his poll tax for a single fiscal year he has kept the matter a profound secret."[154]

Culturally, the area known as No Man's Land would develop differently from the rest of Louisiana. On the surface, the culture of the region should be like that of North Louisiana, which was mostly influenced by Americans, more than the French-influenced southeast Louisiana. However, it doesn't take long to realize that the region is different, with many cultural groups and traditions that set it apart. Locals are very proud of their heritage and quick to point out that they are from the Neutral Strip. Most communities have some type of festival celebrating their culture. While the outlaw culture tends to get the most attention, the region's reputation as a tough and isolated place may better explain its development. People had to become tough in order to survive in this tough land, and anyone not willing to fight hardships, nature or other men to survive would not last long. Many came to No Man's Land not for the chance to live without law, as some outsiders suggest, but to find isolation where they could maintain their culture and be left alone by the outside world. This isolated region gave them a chance to preserve their way of life in ways that other areas did not. Keagan LeJeune may have written one of the best summaries of what No Man's Land is, even two hundred years after the Neutral Strip era ended: "Slow to be settled and marked by a pivotal moment in history, the Neutral Strip region exhibits a culture colored by several pockets of diverse folk groups—like American Indians, remnants of early Spanish colonies,

Scots-Irish pioneers, African Americans, and others—who fiercely hold on to their traditions and notions of identity."[155]

It would take over a century for No Man's Land to truly become Americanized, and "outsiders" often looked down on the poor, rough settlers, but many residents are still proud of their history, heritage and culture. Many feel a great sense of pride in their ancestors' ability to survive and thrive in this lawless region. Many longtime residents still tell stories of outlaws, settlers, treasure hunters and ghosts at family gatherings as if they happened yesterday.

NOTES

Chapter 1

1. Dufour, *Ten Flags*, 122–23.
2. Ibid., 123–25.
3. Slavery and Remembrance, "Haiti (Saint-Domingue)."
4. Marshall, *Western Boundary*, 3–9.
5. Dufour, *Ten Flags*, 132–33.
6. Marshal, *Western Boundary*, 17–19.
7. Miller, "History of Fort Claiborne," 1–4.
8. Miller, "American Troops Arrive," 5.
9. Casey, *Encyclopedia of Forts*, 46.
10. Ibid., 8–11.
11. Marshal, *Western Boundary*, 19–20.

Chapter 2

12. Marshal, *Western Boundary*, 27–28.
13. Leckie, *Sea to Shining Sea*, 242–44; Linklater, *Artist in Treason*, 8.
14. Fredriksen, *American Military Leaders*, 873–74.
15. Ibid., 874.
16. Ibid.
17. Marler, *Neutral Zone*, 39–41.

18. Marshal, *Western Boundary*, 28–29.
19. Linklater, *Artist in Treason*, 202–56.
20. Marshal, *Western Boundary*, 30.

Chapter 3

21. Marler, *Neutral Zone*, 140.
22. Smith, *Good Home*, 40–41.
23. Ibid., 33.
24. Belisle, *History of Sabine Parish*, 62.
25. McCann, "Neutral Strip Revisited."
26. Chipman, *Spanish Texas*, 228; Lytle, "Louisiana's Military Frontier," 7.
27. Lejeune, *Legendary Louisiana Outlaws*, 17–20.
28. Ibid., 26–30; Marler, *Neutral Zone*, 98–101.
29. Lejeune, *Louisiana Outlaws*, 32–33; Davis, *Three Roads*, 52–53.
30. Marler, *Neutral Zone*, 141–42.
31. Nardini, *No Man's Land*, 85.
32. Miller, "History of Fort Claiborne," 35.
33. Ibid., 37–39.
34. Lytle, "Louisiana's Military Frontier," 7–10.
35. Miller, "History of Fort Claiborne," 40–44.
36. Ibid., 43; Chipman, *Spanish Texas*, 228–29.
37. Lytle, "Louisiana's Military Frontier," 9.
38. Ibid., 10.
39. Marshal, *Western Boundary*, 46–47.
40. Lytle, "Louisiana's Military Frontier," 10–11.
41. Ibid., 12.
42. Ibid., 10.
43. Casey, *Encyclopedia*, 185–86, 189.
44. Middleton, "Frontier Outpost," 39.
45. Ibid., 40.
46. Ibid.
47. *Albany (NY) Gazette*, July 19, 1819.
48. Lytle, "Louisiana's Military Frontier," 13–16; Chipman, *Spanish Texas*, 240.
49. Miller, "History of Fort Claiborne," 176.
50. Lytle, "Louisiana's Military Frontier," 16.

Chapter 4

51. LeJeune, *Western Louisiana's Neutral Strip*, 3–4.
52. Couser, "Atakapa Indians."
53. Girard, *Caddos*, 41–107.
54. Middleton, "Frontier Outpost," 15–16.
55. Ibid., 17.
56. Girard, *Caddos*, 107.
57. LeJeune, *Western Louisiana's Neutral Strip*, 6.
58. Ibid., 7.
59. LeJeune, *Western Louisiana's Neutral Strip*, 4–5; Miller, "History of Fort Claiborne," 38–39; Avery, "Spanish in Northwest Louisiana," 223–24.
60. Smith, *Good Home*, 32; Hardin, *Northwestern Louisiana*, 172; Avery, *Annual Report*, 41.
61. Smith, *Good Home*, 33.
62. Pleasant and Pleasant, "Village of Adaes," 1–2, 20.
63. Ibid., 10–11.
64. Ibid., 15.
65. Ibid.
66. Ibid., 16.
67. Ibid., 13.
68. Van Rheenen, "Ethnic Identity," 6–7, 12.
69. Ibid., 8–11.
70. LeJeune, *Western Louisiana's Neutral Strip*, 6–7.
71. Miller, "History of Fort Claiborne," 31–33; Teal, "Underground Railroad Route," 9.
72. Marler, *Neutral Zone*, 101–2.
73. LeJeune, *Louisiana Outlaws*, 33.
74. Ibid., 32–33.
75. Ericson, *Natchitoches Neighbors*, iv; Smith, *Good Home*, 38.

Chapter 5

76. Miller, "History of Fort Claiborne," 160–76.
77. Casey, *Encyclopedia*, 93.
78. Lytle, "Louisiana's Military Frontier," 19; FJHC Book M, 16.
79. DeBose, *Fort Jesup*, 28–31, 108.
80. Gray, *Old Soldier's Story*, 49.

81. *FJHC* Book 1, 5, Casey, *Encyclopedia of Forts*, 94; DeBose, *Fort Jesup*, 51–52, 84–85, 57.

82. DeBose, *Fort Jesup*, 52, 73.

83. Ibid., 54–55; McKay, "Midkiffs," 5.

84. Casey, *Encyclopedia of Forts*, 95; DeBose, *Fort Jesup*, 61–64; Middleton, "Frontier Outpost," 68–69.

85. *FJHC* Book 3, 37.

86. Ibid., 40.

87. Ibid., 43–44.

88. Belisle, *Sabine Parish*, 81.

89. Ibid.

90. Smithwick, "Redlands."

91. Casey, *Encyclopedia of Forts*, 5–6.

92. Smithwick, "Redlands."

93. LeJeune, *Western Louisiana's Neutral Strip*, 7–8.

94. Ibid., 4–5B; Smith, *Good Home*, 63.

95. LeJeune, *Western Louisiana's Neutral Strip*, 4–5B.

96. Ibid., 6B.

97. Marler, *Neutral Zone*, 113–14; Nardini, *No Man's Land*, 89; Durham and Durham, *No Man's Land Pioneers*, 118–20.

98. Marler, *Neutral Zone*, 114–15; Nardini, *No Man's Land*, 91.

99. Isbell, "Land Pirate," 3; Robertson, "Robber John Murrell."

100. Robertson, "Robber John Murrell," 2–3; Marler, *Neutral Zone*, 115–16.

101. Marler, *Neutral Zone*, 6–7; Cuthbertson, "Regulator-Moderator War."

102. *Daily Picayune* (New Orleans, LA), July 29, 1842; Marler, *Neutral Zone*, 140–41; McKay, "Midkiffs."

103. LeJeune, *Western Louisiana's Neutral Strip*, 2C.

104. Ibid., 3C.

105. DeBose, *Fort Jesup*, 103–29.

106. LeJeune, *Western Louisiana's Neutral Strip*, 7–8; Marler, *Neutral Zone*, 147–49.

107. Marler, *Neutral Zone*, 140.

Chapter 6

108. Belisile, *Sabine Parish*, 93.

109. Wilbur, *Home Building and Woodworking*, 6–27.

110. Lacour-Gayet, *Everyday Life*, 39–45.

111. Noel Hume, *Artifacts of Colonial America*, 98–144.
112. Hume, *Artifacts of Colonial America*, 97–98; Gilgun, *Tidings*, 194; McCallum, *Old Sturbridge Village*, 27–28.
113. Gilgun, *Tidings*, 33–70.
114. For a complete description of both civilian and military clothing of the era, see Robert J. Moore Jr.'s *Lewis and Clark: Tailor Made, Trail Worn: Army Life, Clothing and Weapons of the Corps of Discovery* (Helena, MT: Farcountry Press, 2003).
115. Gilgun, *Tidings*, 119–36.
116. McCallum, *Old Sturbridge Village*, 50–51.
117. Nardini, *No Man's Land*, 111–12.
118. Belisle, *Sabine Parish*, 86–87.
119. LeJeune, *Western Louisiana's Neutral Strip*, 2.
120. Marler, *Neutral Zone*, 84.
121. Ibid., 85–86.
122. Ibid., 86–87.
123. LeJeune, *Western Louisiana's Neutral Strip*, 12; Durham and Durham, *No Man's Land Pioneers*, 158.
124. Van Rheenen, "Ethnic Identity," 1.

Chapter 7

125. Marler, *Neutral Zone*, 205–7.
126. Van Rheenen, "Ethnic Identity," 18.
127. Marler, *Neutral Zone*, 125.
128. Ibid., 125–26.
129. Ibid., 142.
130. Ibid., 107–8.
131. Ibid., 108.
132. Ibid., 107, 109.
133. Ibid., 109–10.
134. Ibid., 144.
135. Ibid., 191.
136. Ibid., 192.
137. Ibid.
138. Ibid., 192–93.
139. Van Rheenen, "Ethnic Identity," 2–3.
140. Ibid., 19–20.

Chapter 8

141. Calcasieu Parish Police Jury, "History of Calcasieu Parish"; Cormier, "Timeline History."

142. Calcasieu Parish Police Jury, "History of Calcasieu Parish"; Cormier, "Timeline History."

143. Hardin, *Northwestern Louisiana*, 173; Touchstone, *Sabine Parish History*, 72, 89–90.

144. Hardin, *Northwestern Louisiana*, 177.

145. Ibid., 161.

146. Cameron Parish Police Jury, "Parish History."

147. Smith, *Good Home*, 84–107.

148. Ibid., 200; Casey, *Encyclopedia*, 164.

149. Beauregard Clerk of Court, "Historical Sketch."

150. Holland, *Beauregard and Allen Parishes*, 4–5.

151. Ibid., 7; Beauregard Clerk of Court, "Historical Sketch."

152. Holland, *Beauregard and Allen Parishes*, 8–9.

153. Marler, *Neutral Zone*, 207–8, 210; LeJeune, *Louisiana Outlaws*, 17, 71.

154. Belisle, *Sabine Parish*, 62.

155. LeJeune, "Western Louisiana's Neutral Strip," 1.

BIBLIOGRAPHY

Primary Sources

Albany (NY) Gazette, July 19, 1819. Transcription by Dee McCann, in possession of the author.

Avery, George. *Los Adaes Station Archaeology Program 1999 Annual Report: Appendix 1, Research Design.* Baton Rouge: Louisiana Department of Culture, Recreation and Tourism, Office of Cultural Development, Division of Archaeology, 1999.

Daily Picayune (New Orleans), July 29, 1842.

Fort Jesup Historic Collection (FJHC). 5 vols. On file at Fort Jesup State Historic Site.

Gray, Charles Martin. *The Old Soldiers Story: Autobiography of Charles Martin Gray, Co. A, 7ᵗʰ Regiment, United States Infantry, Embracing Interesting and Exciting Incidents of Army Life on the Frontier, in the Early Part of the Present Century.* Edgefield, SC: Edgefield Advertiser, 1868. Copied from the collections in the Center for American History, University of Texas at Austin.

Smithwick, Noah. "Sojourn in the Redlands." *Dallas Morning News*, June 6, 1897. Transcription by Dee McCann, copy in the author's possession.

Secondary Sources

Avery, George. "The Spanish in Northwest Louisiana 1721–1773." In *Archaeology of Louisiana*. Edited by Mark A. Rees. Baton Rouge: Louisiana State University Press, 2010.

Belisle, John G. *History of Sabine Parish, Louisiana.* Many, LA: Sabine Banner Press, 1912.

Casey, Powell A. *Encyclopedia of Forts, Posts, Named Camps, and Other Military Installations in Louisiana: 1700–1981.* Baton Rouge, LA: Claitor's, 1983.

Chipman, Donald E. *Spanish Texas, 1519–1821.* Austin: University of Texas Press, 1992.

Davis, William C. *Three Roads to the Alamo.* New York: Harper Perennial, 1998.

DeBose, Scott. *Fort Jesup: A History.* Charleston, SC: The History Press, 2022.

Dufour, Charles L. *Ten Flags in the Wind: The Story of Louisiana.* New York: Harper and Row, 1967.

Durham, Marcus, and Rosemary Durham. *No Man's Land Pioneers: Louisiana's Wild, Wild, West.* Tulsa, OK: Realm Research, 2019.

Ericson, Carolyn. *Natchitoches Neighbors in the Neutral Strip.* Nacogdoches, TX: Ericson Books, n.d.

Fredriksen, John C. *American Military Leaders: From Colonial Times to the Present.* Vol. 2. Santa Barbara, CA: ABC-CLJO, 1999.

Gilgun, Beth. *Tidings from the 18th Century.* Texarkana, TX: Scurlock Publishing, 1993.

Girard, Jeffery. *The Caddos and Their Ancestors: Archaeology and the Native People of Northwest Louisiana.* Baton Rouge: Louisiana State University Press, 2018.

Hardin, J. Fair. *Northwestern Louisiana: A History of the Watershed of the Red River, 1714–1937.* Louisville, KY: Historical Record Association, n.d. (late 1930s or early 1940s).

Holland, Charles Wilbur. "The Physiography of Beauregard and Allen Parishes." Unpublished master's thesis, Louisiana State University, 1943.

Isbell, Terry. "The Land Pirate of the Free State." *Old Natchitoches Parish Magazine* 5 (1997): 2–5.

Lacour-Gayet, Robert. *Everyday Life in the United States before the Civil War, 1830–1860.* New York: Frederick Ungar, 1970.

Leckie, Robert. *From Sea to Shining Sea: From the War of 1812 to the Mexican War, The Saga of America's Expansion.* New York: Harper Perennial, 1994.

Lejeune, Keagan. *Legendary Louisiana Outlaws: The Villains and Heroes of Folk Justice.* Baton Rouge: Louisiana State University Press, 2016.

Linklater, Andro. *An Artist in Treason: The Extraordinary Double Life of General James Wilkinson*. New York: Walker, 2009.

Lytle, Richard. "A View on the March of Louisiana's Military Frontier to the Sabine River." Unpublished paper, Northwestern State University, 1998.

Marler, Don C. *The Neutral Zone: Backdoor to the United States*. Woodville, TX: Dogwood Press, 1995.

Marshall, Thomas M. *A History of the Western Boundary of the Louisiana Purchase, 1819–1841*. Berkeley: University of California Press, 1944.

McCallum, Kent. *Old Sturbridge Village*. New York: Harry N. Abrams, 1996.

McCann, Dee. "The Neutral Strip Revisited." *Sabine Index*, November 13, 2013.

McKay, G.M. "The Midkiffs of White County Tennessee." N.p., n.d. Copy provided by Stanley Fletcher.

Middleton, Harry F., Jr. "Frontier Outpost: A History of Fort Jesup, Louisiana, 1822–1846." Unpublished master's thesis, Louisiana State University, 1973.

Miller, Marshal Stone, Jr. "American Troops Arrive in Natchitoches to Take Possession of Territory." *Old Natchitoches Parish Magazine* 31 (1999): 2–8.

———. "The History of Fort Claiborne, Louisiana, 1804–1822." Unpublished master's thesis, Louisiana State University, 1969.

Noel Hume, Ivor. *A Guide to Artifacts of Colonial America*. New York: Alfred A. Knopf, 1976.

Pleasant, Darryl, and Randall Pleasant. "The Village of Adaes: A Nineteenth Century Refugee Settlement in Natchitoches Parish Louisiana." Updated version of an article presented at the 1990 Caddo Conference.

Smith, Steven D. *A Good Home for a Poor Man: Fort Polk and Vernon Parish 1800–1940*. Department of Defense, 1999.

Touchstone, Samuel J. *Sabine Parish History*. Princeton: Folk-Life Books, 1997.

Van Rheenen, Mary B. "'Can You Tell Me Who My People Are?': Ethnic Identity among the Hispanic-Indian People of Sabine Parish, Louisiana." Unpublished master's thesis, Louisiana State University, 1987.

Wilbur, C. Keith. *Home Building and Woodworking in Colonial America*. Guilford, CT: Globe Pequot Press, 1992.

Online Resources

Beauregard Clerk of Court. "Historical Sketch." https://www.beauregard clerk.org/historical-beauregard.

Calcasieu Parish Police Jury. "History of Calcasieu Parish." https://www. calcasieu.gov/government/parish-history.

———. "Parish History." https://cameronpj.org/parish-history.

Cormier, Adley. "A Timeline History of Lake Charles and Southwest Louisiana. Calcasieu Historical Preservation Society." November 17, 2007. https://calcasieupreservation.com/index.php?option=com_conte nt&view=article&id=2&Itemid=186.

Couser, Dorothy. "Atakapa Indians." Handbook of Texas Online, published by the Texas State Historical Association, originally published 1976, updated July 1, 1995. https://www.tshaonline.org/handbook/entries/atakapa-indians.

Cuthbertson, Gilbert M. "Regulator-Moderator War." Handbook of Texas Online, published by the Texas State Historical Association, July 2, 2019. https://www.tshaonline.org/handbook/entries/regulator-moderator-war.

LeJeune, Keagan. "Western Louisiana's Neutral Strip: Its History, People, and Legends." Folklife in Louisiana. https://www.louisianafolklife.org/LT/Articles_Essays/nslejeune1.html.

Robertson, Rickey. "The Robber John Murrell and His Famous Hideouts (November 2012)." Center for Regional Heritage Research, Stephen F. Austin State University of Texas. https://www.sfasu.edu/heritagecenter/5818.asp.

Slavery and Remembrance. "Haiti (Saint-Domingue)." https://slaveryand remembrance.org/articles/article/?id=A0111.

Teal, Rolonda. "Underground Railroad Route along El Camino Real de las Tejas." National Park Service, July 2010. https://www.nps.gov/elte/learn/historyculture/upload/Underground-Railroad-Route-along-the-Camino-508.pdf.

ABOUT THE AUTHOR

S cott DeBose has spent most of his life living in No Man's Land. He became interested in the history of the region at an early age, listening to stories of outlaws and treasures. DeBose spent several years working at Fort Jesup State Historic Site in college; he now serves as the president of the Friends of Fort Jesup Inc. and was involved in the No Man's Land Bicentennial Celebration at Fort Jesup in 2019. This is DeBose's second book published by The History Press; his first was *Fort Jesup: A History* (2022). DeBose holds a bachelor of arts in history and anthropology and a master's in music. He lives in Many, Louisiana, with his wife and four children, where he serves as director of bands at Many Junior High and High School.

Visit us at
www.historypress.com